Radical Simplicity

RADICAL SIMPLICITY

CREATING AN AUTHENTIC LIFE

by DAN PRICE

9   8   7   6   5   4   3   2   1
Digit on the right indicates the number of this printing

Library of Congress Control Number 2005902522
ISBN–13: 978-0-7624-2492-4
ISBN–10: 0-7624-2492-3

Cover and Interior designed by Doogie Horner
Illustrated by Dan Price
Edited by Deborah Grandinetti
Typography: Ardley's Hand, Bakserville, Block, and Bulldog

Quote on page 121 by Herman Hesse, from SIDDHARTHA, copyright 1951 by New Directions Publishing Corp. Reprinted by permission of New Directions Publishing Corp.

This book may be ordered by mail from the publisher.
Please include $2.50 for postage and handling.
But try your bookstore first!

Running Press Book Publishers
125 South Twenty-second Street
Philadelphia, Pennsylvania 19103-4399

Visit us on the web!
www.runningpress.com
www.moonlight-chronicles.com

CONTENTS

Intro 06

Chapter One:
FROM CAVES TO CONDOS 12

Chapter Two:
THE LONG ROAD HOME 24

Chapter Three:
HOME IS WHERE THE HOBO IS 38

Chapter Four:
DOMICILES, DUNGAREES, AND DISCOVERY 54

Chapter Five:
TIPIS, TENTS, AND TRAVEL 72

Chapter Six:
OF HOBBITS HOLES AND THIEVES 100

Chapter Seven:
LIFE IN THE MEADOW 120

Chapter Eight:
THE END OF THE BEGINNINGS 144

INTRODUCTION

"To live within limits. To want one thing. Or a few things very much and love them dearly. Cling to them, survey them from every angle. Become one with them—that is what makes the poet, the artist, the human being."

Johann Goethe

...the cabin I built in 1972

I was one lucky kid. Lucky because I lived at the base of a huge, forested mountain covered with old dirt roads and ancient Indian trails. After the enslavement of each long school day, I would run off into those deep, dark woods afoot or tear into them on my Honda 90. Just roaming around. Dreaming of a freedom-filled future. And endlessly building hideaways of all kinds.

Some old, lingering vision was haunting me. I was convinced that one day I would live inside the trunk of a gigantic mossy tree, just like a squirrel. Or deep underground like Peter Pan's lost boys, among gnarly roots. I built regardless of the weather: little rock huts. Lean-tos of dead trees, covered with spicy-smelling fir boughs. Earthbound hovels. And even a 5 x 8 cabin that I built in great secrecy when I was barely 16 years old. I was convinced my father wouldn't approve, so I snuck a chainsaw and nails from his shop. But toward the end of construction, the five kids in my family found out and they all helped carry the roof boards up the steep hill to finish the project.

These days, nearing the age of 50, I'm still haunted by those dreams of solitude and simplicity. When I'm hiking in the woods, my radar is on, constantly on the lookout for the best camping spot or cave or cliff face that could be turned into a secret shelter.

old tent

In 1990 I came across a pristine 2-acre meadow in Eastern Oregon and began over 14 years of experimentation in alternative living spaces that included tipis, huts, sheds, and mountaineering tents.

new tent!

For the last three years I have inhabited an 80-square-foot circular pine-paneled room that is dug into a hillside and 2 feet underground. There's a skylight that I can open for illumination and fresh air, soft carpeting, electric light, hotplate and radio, non-perishable food, a roll-up sleeping pad that also serves as a seat, books, telephone, a small shelf for

the underground room

clothes, and a mini ceramic heater. The door is tiny and I must crawl through on hands and knees, which despite my 6-foot frame feels appropriate, since each coming and going from such a warm, dry shelter ought to be a reverant act. Everything in the room is within arm's reach! Nothing ever becomes misplaced or lost. And the tiny space offers complete silence, which is great for deep, creative sleeping.

Outside lies a beautiful old horse pasture ringed with trees of all kinds. Since 1990 I have leased the two acres for $100 a year. I've made improvements by clearing brush, cleaning up downed trees and removing weeds, and planting new grass seed.

There's a small hillside garden, a propane-powered sauna next to a gurgling stream, and a narrow trail heading northward that leads to town a mere six blocks away.

the tipi days!

My longtime partner Lynne and our two children Shane and Shilo live six miles away, and I sometimes spend time with them in their conventional home. In the early 90s they spent several summers living in the tipi, but I couldn't convince them that simple living was a viable option. Going back and forth between modern and primitive living has given me the opportunity to live in both worlds, leading to interesting comparisons and conclusions.

I definitely prefer living a more primitive lifestyle where I'm not hogtied and surrounded by the endless tasks and financial black holes of keeping a full-blown household up and running. In the meadow it's as if I've stepped back a few hundred years. The days move quietly along in a natural way. Sometimes my old car is parked for weeks down at the end of the road. I may not go into town for days, being perfectly content to just work in the garden, watch the ant nest, read a fascinating book, hike upriver for a midday plunge in the big pond, or work up the mail to fill all the orders for the little illustrated journal I've been sending out to like-minded folks ever since my simple living project began.

I continually try to express my thankfulness to the landowners who have allowed me to run through countless crazy experiments in living these last 14 years. My main focus all along has been to somehow dodge all those lassoes being thrown by that darned cowboy called life. So many people these days seem to be entangled in his long twisting rope! Instead, I'm trying to ignore all the societal pressures that try to define who I'm supposed to be or what "success" means. I'd like to just honor our sacred earth by becoming so small, so quiet, and so unsubstantial that the environment I inhabit feels barely a whisper of my small existence, just a wafting spirit drifting through the trees. In this way, nature is free to express itself fully while I try to comprehend and appreciate its vast universal rhythms.

Here on the raggedy edge of the 21st century, with nations warring and humans crisscrossing the globe like frightened jackrabbits, forever in search of some sense of happiness and security, there's still much to be learned by simply questioning all the assumptions about the lifestyles that society handed each of us at birth.

Important new discoveries are waiting to be made. These discoveries do not lie in the ever-expanding "information" we are all gathering. I believe that long ago, man abandoned and forgot all he ever really needed to know about living a harmonious life with the earth. But if we are able to awaken to what is essential for our happiness, there's still hope that each of us may lead an authentic life.

And that's what I've spent my own lifetime trying to achieve. To be a healthy, happy, and most important, *free* human being, able to pursue most of the creative interests that come my way. This is the story of how one person found true freedom right here in America. And how a stress-free lifestyle can be had by anyone with the desire to live the dream.

near the ponds.

FROM CAVES TO CONDOS

"THE VERY SIMPLICITY AND NAKEDNESS of man's life in the primitive ages imply this advantage at least, that they left him still but a sojourner in nature. When he was refreshed with food and sleep he contemplated his journey again. He dwelt, as it were, in a tent in this world, and was either threading the valleys, or crossing the plains, or climbing the mountaintops. But lo! men have become the tools of their tools. The man who independently plucked the fruits when he was hungry is become a farmer; and he who stood under a tree for shelter, a housekeeper. We now no longer camp as for a night, but have settled down on earth and forgotten heaven."

—Henry David Thoreau, *Walden*

For the most part, my earliest years are a complete blank. However, one memory does stand out. Our family was living in a big sprawling house in a town called Orting in the state of Washington. I wasn't in school yet, so I must have been less than 6 years old. I remember wandering one day through some tall grass and discovering an abandoned chicken coop nearby. It was a small space with a squeaky wooden door. As I walked in, my movements raised a silty dust cloud. Sitting inside, I thought that with a little cleaning up, this would be a way better place to live than our stupid old house.

Another bright memory. I'm in another house, in the 60s. I can hear a Beatles album playing in the living room. Crawling out of bed, I go to the nearest wall, which has three cupboards built into it. By opening the latch of each cupboard door I'm able to climb them like stairs in my stocking feet and enter a long, dark storage area at the top. Inside I've hidden blankets, a pillow, and a flashlight. In I go with a soft click of the door behind me. And it's in that small space in the darkness that I finish my Saturday morning sleep. In my hideaway no one can find me. I have become invisible and experience a profound sense of safety and security.

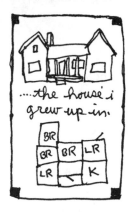

....the house i grew up in.

Before finding that secret storage space, I would surround the lower portion of my bunk bed with hanging blankets, creating an enclosed sleeping room. Again, I enjoyed the privacy and loved having my own tiny space.

In later years my brothers and I dug a big hole 4 feet deep out behind the house, covered it with plywood and dirt, then roasted some foil-wrapped potatoes in a fireplace carved out of one wall. I can still remember the smell of the earth and how it got all over my backside as I slid down the doorway chute into the hole. I think we all enjoyed the thought of creating our own place and leaving the house we called home behind.

That feeling has never left me and has kept me scribbling endless unusual house plans and building hideaways my whole life. In one sense it feels like there is something pulling at my very innards: a strange, age-old desire to return to the past. To live the way man did before the Industrial Revolution, before he began to live in villages and then cities. Perhaps even back to the hunter-gatherer days when man wandered free as a nomad.

In one sense it feels like there is something pulling at my very innards: a strange, age-old desire to return to the past.

To find some answers to these deep longings and desires that have kept me perplexed in our immobilizing consumer society, I began to

study the Native American culture that used to inhabit the valley where I live. The Nez Perce Indians fished salmon from the local rivers, gathered roots and berries, and hunted deer and elk for meat. I tried hard to assimilate their moral values after reading of their wise ways. I could appreciate the concept of considering the consequences of your actions seven generations down the line. If decisions you're making now would adversely affect future people, you change your plan.

I was also in awe of the fact that all those generations of Indians who lived here in this beautiful setting left only a few stone tools and arrowheads as evidence. Because they lived in light tipis, concrete was never poured. Because they led semi-nomadic lives, fences were never built. Because they ate only what nature provided, crops were never grown. But then white settlers came to this valley in the early 1870s. In the short time since then, we who booted the Indians right out of their own homelands, not just here but all over North America, have commenced to pour enough concrete to cover the entire globe, stretched millions of miles of barbed wire that traps deer

Nowadays you can stand here or nearly anywhere in America and be assaulted by the over-building, the sprawl. . .

and geometrically divides the naturally rolling landscape, run endless telephone and electrical lines that pollute the pristine views, and spewed chemicals everywhere in order to decide what will and what won't grow. All this in just over 100 years.

then...

...and now

(What were their days like 500 or 1,000 years ago? Did they have desires like ours?)

Nowadays you can stand here or nearly anywhere in America and be assaulted by the over-building, the sprawl, the general messiness and ugly weed-like growth of our highly industrialized society. I recently rode a tricycle across the country, and well remember the literally hundreds of miles of strip malls on Florida's gulf coast. During the most recent hurricane season I secretly hoped that the storms would wash the entire place clean of all the manmade mess that had accumulated there!

And then I think back to what the Native Americans left after *thousands* of years of habitation and I have to wonder. What in the hell are we modern-day humans up to anyway?

I have a neighbor friend with whom I spend a lot of late nights in the sauna. We try to stretch our imaginations and wonder just what this place looked like before the white man came. We can see deep horse trails winding up and down the rocky valley and big white tipis poking their spiky tops over the brown hills up at the lake. We also wonder what it was like to actually be an Indian. What were their days like 500 or 1,000 years ago?

(17)

Turning the keys in an ignition or walking a few steps from the car into the office

Did they have desires like ours? Did they dream of better lives or were they mostly content? Perhaps they were filled with a kind of happiness that we humans living today will never know. An Indian's acute knowledge of the land, and the fact that art was a part of everything he did, must have led to a very fulfilling life.

Amid all the heat and steam, my friend and I also talk at length about the animals we see here. And we wonder exactly how and why man evolved from his primitive state to a world-conquering warrior. We know that the deer has certainly evolved somewhat over many years, yet still has no need for fingers or the ability to walk upright, since all the food it needs is at its feet. Man, on the other hand, was lucky enough to have apes as his ancestors—animals that already had long arms and fingers and occasionally walked upright. This enabled early man to manipulate his environment and make tools to better his life. Eventually he was able to do amazing spiraling double back flips and land on two feet without a bobble, as we've seen in recent Olympics. That shows how man's coordination can develop rapidly with practice. Unfortunately our lifestyle doesn't require us to be fast runners to catch game the way we used to. We only need to be capable of the easiest motor skills to get along. Turning the keys in an ignition or walking a few steps from the car into the office seem to suffice. So my friend and I ask one another the question while sitting in the swirling steam: Is man actually de-evolving? Are we becoming less smart than our ancestors?

Jared Diamond thinks so. In his Pulitzer Prize-winning book *Guns, Germs, and Steel,* he compares the differences between so-called "primitive" New Guinea children who spend their entire lives living intimately with nature and American children who grow up with Game Boys in their hands. Guess who he thinks have sharper minds and the ability to learn new concepts more quickly!

Since learning about the lifestyles of the Nez Perce I continued to come across quotes that seem quite unbelievable, such as this one by the late Paul Shepherd:

> Cultural man has been on the earth for over two million years. For 99 percent of this period he lived as a hunter-gatherer. Only in the last 10,000 years has he begun to domesticate plants and animals.

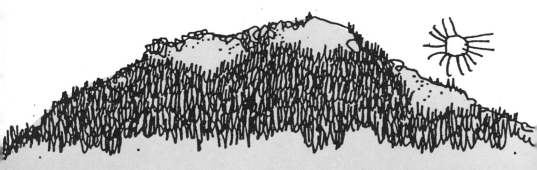

How could this be true? On I studied, trying to get a better grasp of the "bigger" picture. Where had man come from and how long has he been tramping around the earth? I wanted to know actual timeframes so I could position myself in the greater record of history, instead of just my own lifespan. Here are some of the amazing and mindboggling things I discovered.

1. According to current scientific thinking, the human evolutionary line diverged from African chimpanzees and gorillas between ten and five million years ago.

2. The most primitive tool-using humans emerged in East Africa 2.5 million years ago.

3. Archeological studies begin with the first preserved evidence of human activity 2.5 million years ago.

4. For 99.8 percent of those 2.5 million years, man survived as a hunter-gatherer!

5. Humans eventually colonized the entire globe with their expert toolmaking abilities and fluent speech. This revolution took place against a backdrop of constant and widespread climatic change, when the world was a very different place than it is today.

6. The discovery of fire occurred about 1.5 million years ago and was a major breakthrough in man's mastery of the environment.

7. The earliest known representational art—cave paintings, rock engravings, and decorated objects—are about 30,000 years old.

8. The Americas are believed to have been populated around 15,000 years ago during the last Ice Age when ocean levels were low enough to allow Asiatic humans to cross the land bridge of the Bering Sea. These new inhabitants spent the next 5,000 years as hunter-gatherers before the advent of farming.

9. Ten thousand years ago the end of the last Ice Age caused the farthest-reaching changes in man's economy ever experienced. A mere 5,000 years later, the domestication of plants and animals was widespread. Farmers and herders established themselves throughout the entire Old World.

10. Before 10,000 years ago, there were no human settlements approaching the size of a small town.

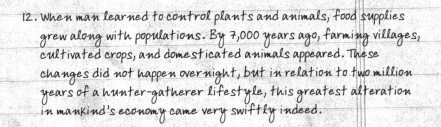

11. Nine thousand years ago, near an oasis by the Dead Sea, the first human settlement began. An exterior wall surrounding circular huts became known as Jericho.

12. When man learned to control plants and animals, food supplies grew along with populations. By 7,000 years ago, farming villages, cultivated crops, and domesticated animals appeared. These changes did not happen overnight, but in relation to two million years of a hunter-gatherer lifestyle, this greatest alteration in mankind's economy came very swiftly indeed.

13. All six billion of us living today are actually blood relatives. One scientist gives the rough estimate that the original Eve would be our ten-thousandth great-grandmother!

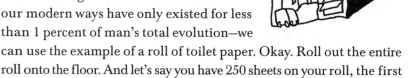

In order to conceptualize what to me is the most amazing detail of all—the fact that our modern ways have only existed for less than 1 percent of man's total evolution—we can use the example of a roll of toilet paper. Okay. Roll out the entire roll onto the floor. And let's say you have 250 sheets on your roll, the first sheets representing present day, with each successive sheet going further and further into the past, okay? Well, within that very first sheet lies ALL of man's history! And the remaining 249 sheets contain the earth's ENTIRE history! So let's get a grip here on our so-called importance on the big spinning rock, could we?

So. After all my investigating I can see where my tiny self fits into the enormous scheme of man's progress from the very beginning. I am able to get a handle on how long all our recent crazymaking has gone on. Kind of like when you study books on geology and come to realize that the rocks you are sitting on next to a river are some 3.5 billion years old! And realizing that whole continents have actually MOVED! And mountain ranges have RISEN! And knowing that the

light you now see emanating from a distant star began its journey long before you were EVEN BORN! These are the kinds of realizations that can open our eyes to a broader reality. It can cause you to see your own supposed problems in a whole new light and from a larger perspective.

With all these new realizations I still have questions. If man has actually lived the life of a free nomadic hunter-gatherer for over 99 percent of his time on earth, where did all the societal concepts come from that so quickly got the masses marching in lockstep? Why are so few simpler lifestyles deemed normal in this sped-up world?

I believe we were all put here to discover our own truths and honor them to the fullest. I don't believe that man went through eons of evolution to become lemmings or sheep. Each and every one of us has a unique spirit that is begging to be nurtured. Maybe nurturing that spirit would truly evolve our species.

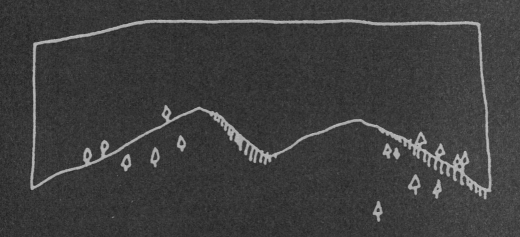

THE LONG ROAD HOME

"NOBODY IS MORE FLEXIBLE AND ADAPTABLE than the person who has nothing. He can turn left or right, lie down or run on, and his life overall will continue little changed. But let the average member of society change direction or lose stride and he will be out of a job, then lose the car, and not much later be out of his house. It is no wonder that we want so desperately to keep going as we are, lest one false step lead to the collapse of our whole house-of-cards."

—Ferenc Mate

After marrying Lynne, my high school sweetheart, I spent most of the 1980s shooting photographs for small-town newspapers in five different states. The majority of those years were in the bluegrass state of Kentucky, where we lived with our two children in a small house on Pumpkin Run Road. As the name implies, it was idyllic: rolling green hills with a one-lane stretch of pavement snaking back into the hollow to our house. We bought 5 acres of hillside, with weeping willows, a pond, and wonderfully friendly neighbors. And although we loved that place to death we'd still stay up late at night drawing exotic plans for our ultimate dream house.

We had made it our quest to rethink all the usual layouts and taken-for-granted rooms in a regular house. We wondered if a big bedroom was really necessary, or could we build a cozy cubbyhole into a wall instead. And why did everyone haul his or her clothes back and forth from bedrooms to the washroom, when a centralized washroom/clothes storage area right next to the bathroom might suffice? This "garment station" idea seemed unique at the time. Now that our kids are privacy loving teens, we're not so sure it would work.

Unfortunately, the income of a small-town news photographer does not even come close to

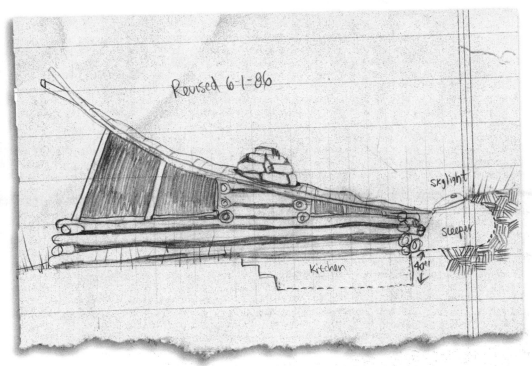

Revised 6-1-86

skylight

sleeper

Kitchen

40"

one of my first under-
ground dwelling plans

the amount needed to build dream houses, so the plans were eventually put in a drawer.

Back at the job I spent endless days searching the quiet back roads for interesting characters to photograph and put in the newspaper, which needed at least four feature pictures a day plus a full-page picture story each weekend. My favorite subject matter was the simple rural people who always welcomed me with open arms and seemed to move with an amazing grace through the misty tobacco patches and cornfields. Without realizing it at the time, I think I was actually on the hunt to find mentors, people who could teach me through example how to live at peace in a stressed-out world.

I felt a distinct, deep longing for the lifestyle of old-timers like Lizzy McGafee, whom I visited often and photographed standing in the doorway of her antebellum cabin or sitting by her coal-burning fireplace.

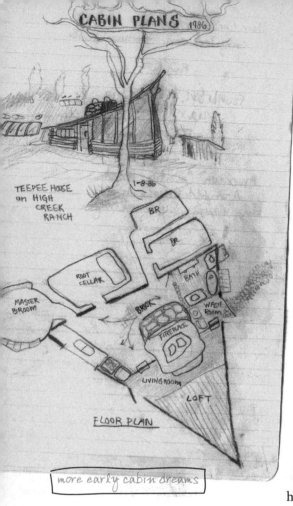

CABIN PLANS 1986

TEEPEE HOUSE
on HIGH
CREEK
RANCH

1-8-86

BR

BR

ROOT
CELLAR

BATH

MASTER
BEDROOM

BRICK

WASH
ROOM

FIREPLACE

LIVING ROOM

LOFT

FLOOR PLAN

more early cabin dreams

She had been born in that one room and had spent her entire life rarely venturing beyond the nearby county line! I really envied her slow-paced lifestyle, which seemed so serene compared to my daily deadlines and worry-filled existence.

A similar feeling arose when I spent time among the South Fork Mennonites, who lived as a small, self-sufficient farming community. These people had chosen to live without modern-day amenities and were happy and deeply religious. Whenever I could spare a free day I'd speed off in my old car to Casey County to be among those quiet souls who spent their days doing hard hand labor in their crop-filled fields. Sometimes I would be invited to their robust midday meal, where I witnessed a multitude of homegrown foods being devoured and plates being cleaned with slices of thick whole-wheat bread. Back home we discussed the possibility of chucking it all to go live among the Mennonites, but we backed off when we realized we did not share in their Old World religious beliefs. We were also still very young, and enjoyed our stereo and TV, and couldn't imagine living without them.

Lizzy

I really envied Lizzie's slow-paced lifestyle, which seemed so serene compared to my daily deadlines and worry-filled existence.

———————◇———————

We spent many happy years there among those fascinating Kentuckians, until one late summer afternoon when I experienced a sea change. I was following an old chicken farmer back to his barn through a tall, leafy tobacco field when I clicked THIS picture. At that moment I knew that I was done with that segment of my life, finished with looking for all those mysterious characters I had been reading about in Faulkner novels. It was time to return home to Oregon, where the vision of simplicity would continue to grow and become an actual lifestyle.

the last
Kentucky picture

Driving west, I started keeping a daily journal. The car broke down in Utah and had to have its engine rebuilt, so I sat for a week missing my daughter's birthday and thinking about new concepts and ideas. It seemed to me that there were three very important decisions a person had to make in order to be fulfilled and move toward their destiny. These essential decisions can forever affect a person's life in either a negative or positive way. And if one of them hasn't been fully realized and acted on, then the remaining two cannot form a cohesive whole.

THESE THREE VASTLY IMPORTANT CHOICES IN OUR LIVES ARE:

1. WHERE YOU LIVE: Choosing where you would *really* like to live and finding your *true home* seem to be of paramount importance, and not choosing just because you happen to have a job there. It needs to be the place that fulfills your needs and desires in many ways. That one place on earth that you feel connected to. A place you could spend the rest of your life.

2. YOUR PARTNER: Most of us eventually hook up with another person we find drifting on the seas of humanity. *Choosing* that spouse or mate could possibly be the most important decision we ever make. This decision usually reverberates long into our future in unforeseen ways. Once again, we can only hope that the choice creates a positive instead of negative force in our lives.

3. YOUR JOB: This big decision, hopefully, is derived from your *strongest interests* instead of just earning a paycheck. If you seek to turn your favorite hobbies or activities into some sort of job, the chances are great

that you will be happier. There are those who absolutely love their jobs and can't wait to "get back at it." And doesn't it make sense that we should be excited about the one thing we do during such a large portion of our lives? And that just like a good life partner, it stimulates us to better ourselves and everything around us?

Yet in these fast-paced times I often wonder how many people take a gamble and move to a new place just because it makes their heart sing. And when you read recent marriage statistics, doesn't it seem as if more people are getting divorced than married? Plus, how many folks do you know who say they love their jobs? Many feel trapped and unhappy in the work they do but stay with it because so much time or expensive schooling was involved in their career choice. Consider a recent story about how heart attacks happen most often on Monday mornings as the work force heads back to the daily grind.

It would be very interesting to know how much of the population feels fully satisfied during their lives and which of their three choices are positive ones. Which brings me back to my Kentucky story.

My partner and I married when we were young. VERY young. And we moved. Lots! Then all of the sudden we had kids. Yikes! And then we argued. Way too much. So after 10 years we chose to leave Kentucky and go our separate ways. She took the kids to western Oregon to finish getting her degree and I headed for the pine-covered hills of my childhood home with dreams of unbridled minimalism on my mind, and pondered how to reconcile the loss of one of those three essential keys to happiness.

Before leaving Kentucky I threw out or sold all the extraneous items that wouldn't fit in my 1960 Ford Falcon or the 5 boxes I was mailing west. Once I was back in my home state, things really got rolling

along as I became totally smitten with the simplicity concept. Upon arriving, I promptly rented a small cabin by a lake and started taking long walks in the wilderness to clear my head of all that photography noise and plan my next move towards a Thoreauvian lifestyle. I had dreams of living in a tipi on a lonely hill or burrowing into a hillside and living like one of the characters in *The Wind In The Willows*.

my first indie publication, SHOTS.

FLOPHOUSE BATHROOM

Later that fall I moved into a downtown flophouse hotel room that had a great view of the mountains and a cold bathroom down a long, creaking hallway. The room was above the oldest bar in town. The proprietor wore a crooked red wig. The rent was $85 a month!

Leaving my full-time/full-benefits job back in Kentucky was scary, but I brought along a small photo publication that I had founded in 1986 called *Shots*. That 1650-subscriber magazine about "the fine art of photography" kept me busy playing starving independent editor/publisher for the next five years.

I missed my family terribly, and would travel to see them after I mailed off each bi-monthly issue of the magazine to the subscribers. To quell my loneliness I busily searched for a piece of leasable land to somehow live on.

Back in Kentucky, I had read about a man who hated the idea of tying his life to a mortgage. He talked a local farmer into allowing him to build a tiny abode way in the back of the farmer's property. The agreement was that he could live there in peace for $100 a year. If he ever decided to vacate, the house would revert to the farmer.

This sounded like a great idea to me, having never been interested in the intricacies of modern-day shenanigans like car loans or mortgage payments. Soon I placed an ad in the local paper. "Newcomer seeks rural property to lease for tipi habitation." Several tobacco-chewing, hard-bitten ranchers that I went to see said things like, "Ya wanna do what?" and "Well, I just don't see how that would work, young feller!"

As the days wore on and fall became winter, I sat for hours each day in the big rocking chair in my hotel room, making notes and sketches of all the new simple-living ideas I was dreaming up with the help of such pioneers as Henry David Thoreau and Harlan Hubbard. I drew up an Essentials List, which seems pretty ridiculous now, but included all the items I thought I needed to live successfully:

MY MUST-HAVE LIST

- Electricity
- Hot plate
- Microwave
- Refrigerator
- Stereo/TV
- Computer/copier
- Water heater
- Sink
- Toilet
- Shower or tub
- Lights
- Books
- Heater, etc.

I started collecting all the photographs of tipis I could find and glued them in a big scrapbook. The local library had an abundance of books about the Nez Perce Indians, so I read each and every one.

a friend's tipi
near the lake

I talked to people who had lived in tipis. I discussed with several tipi companies the possibility of living year-round in one. During this period I had a vision-like experience. I was driving down a valley road one crisp fall day. On a distant hill I saw a tall white tipi perfectly silhouetted against the Indian summer sky. From that moment on, all I could think of was finding a small plot of land and purchasing a tipi to begin a true experiment in simple living.

❝ Maybe I could live in a tipi in Joseph. The only thing I can't figure out is how I'd get a shower or bath. Everything else would work. It would be very peaceful to live in a tipi. You could just live up on someone's land and not have to buy any. Solar power could run all the stuff. Also, you could move to another place if the situation changed or you got bored. Maybe people would think that I was weird if I lived in a tipi. Maybe the tiny space would get on your nerves. Maybe you would spend lots more time in the outdoors. Maybe it would be very peaceful and satisfying. Maybe I will just do it! ❞

HOME
— IS WHERE —
THE HOBO IS

"THOREAU WISHED SIMPLY TO ILLUSTRATE the increasing subservience of man to property. On the surface he did none of those things which Americans seem required to do. Yet his way of living was distinctly American and he lived with an individuality which catches the American imagination. The life he presents in his book *Walden* became a symbol of the individual freedom on which we like to think the American way of life is based."

—Norman Holmes Pearson

As winter approached I continued making forays into the neighboring woods, searching for some kind of secret hideaway. A cabin caretaker position was available six miles up a steep trail in a local wilderness area where I had snowshoed several times. I tried to imagine living that far removed from society, and in the end decided it probably wouldn't work.

I built a tiny makeshift rock shelter on the shore of the lake. I discovered several abandoned miners' cabins and talked with the Forest Service about resurrecting their shabby remains, but was told that they were historical sites.

Being so new to town, I was a little scared asking complete strangers if I could put a tipi on their land. Then one very cold day in December the perfect place presented itself! I was wandering along the riverside and spied a narrow strip of pastureland that appeared to be detached from any adjoining homes.

BELIEVE IT OR NOT all my searching may have paid off! I have found a wonderfully secret place along the creek with big trees and a flat spot for a tipi. And it's only 2 or 3 hundred yards from the hotel room. I have contacted the owners about the possibility of putting up a summer tent there for a quiet place to read and write. The lady said she would talk to her husband about it. Hope it works out. It's just perfect!

And much to my surprise, the owners said yes a few days later. So we wrote up a contract of sorts, explaining that I would pay them $100 a year, clean up all the downed trees, and repair broken fence lines in the meadow. At this point my nightly drawing journal overflowed with sketches and ideas for the newly discovered site. I dreamed up a wooden floor for the tipi, a concealed sink, and many other house-like amenities. All winter long I drew like a madman and enjoyed the occasional epiphanies that arose from so much hard thinking. By the time spring arrived, my big plans were all laid out and ready for action.

Some of my good friends over the years say that I was extremely lucky to have found such an amazing deal, and I do feel very fortunate, but I think that others with similar ideas could also find land where the owners would agree to such terms. There are endless acres out in the countryside that house nothing but cows. When you're taking to a landowner about your ideas, it's important to present yourself as a clean, respectable, upstanding citizen. The last thing a landowner wants is some loser dragging old cars and other garbage onto their property. Another option: It's legal to camp out in the National Forests if you pick up and move every 14 days or so.

In the spring I made a new friend named Chuck, a local cowboy who had an old tipi for sale. Under that wide-brimmed hat and behind a

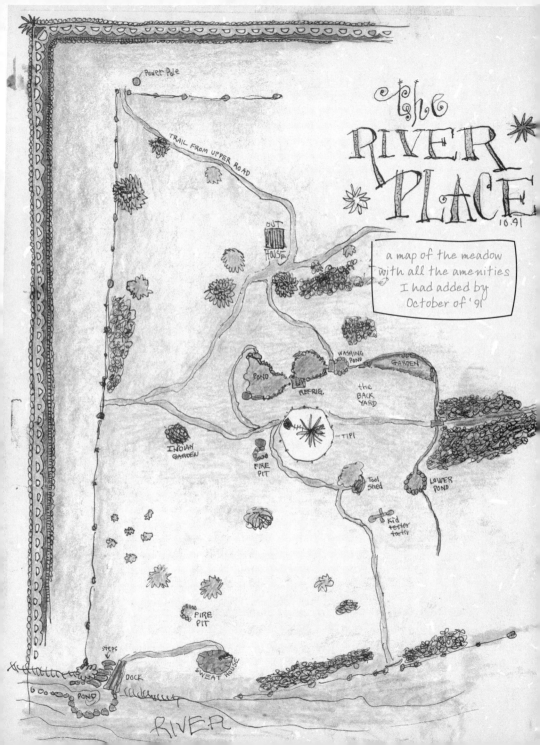

at the first tipi, heating rocks for the sauna

the TRAIL TO TOWN

thick beard a large grin spread when I told him I was hoping to someday live in a tipi fulltime. He commented that he had lived in his and that it was the best time of his whole life.

Because I kept the flophouse room in town, the tipi was to be a place to read, write, and get away from noisy Main Street. I knew I wanted to live there eventually, but still had some reservations about the possibility of doing so.

Within a week I purchased the tipi and drove up into the hills to cut some long skinny poles for the framework. The next day I laid the poles out in the meadow and slowly peeled each one with a grass scythe. Once they had dried in the sun I rubbed on two coats of linseed oil, which sealed the wood and enhanced the color, much as a rock's color deepens when dipped in water.

After visually surveying the meadow, I decided on a flat spot right in the middle of the property that would catch plenty of the midday sun, even in the winter months. I laid down plastic and found a chunk of brown rug for the floor. I cleaned up an old chest of drawers in the hotel room and hauled it to the tipi to store things in. I also brought over a water bottle, cassette player and headphones, and a pile of books, along with journaling supplies.

The first few days and nights in the tipi were absolutely surreal. I guess when you have dreamed of doing something for a long time, then get to actually do it, your mind isn't sure if it is true or it's just your imagination. I remember lying on the mattress at night looking up through the smoke flap hole at the bright stars. And lighting candles and going outside for long periods of time, just staring at the new dwelling. It was one of those things that seemed so beautiful I could scarcely believe it, like staring into the Grand Canyon. Standing and beholding all the beauty of that place is one of the things I still do there. Nature seems to reveal its magic if you are quiet and still. To me the tipi just seems like another part of the meadow, like a tree or a rock. It completes the open space where it stands and looks absolutely natural. In the early days, standing outside in the dark, watching the play of candlelight on the yellowish top poles jutting skyward filled my being with complete happiness all the way from the hair standing up on the back of my neck to my tingling toes in the dewy grass.

There was a day in particular that I remember. Standing by the tipi, just looking all around, I noticed small things like the twitching tail of a squirrel doing his highwire act up in the trees. Families of birds circling out over the river. The way a light breeze herded dry leaves into a low spot. And then everything got very quiet for a while. Listening to the river or maybe those yakking birds, I didn't realize how still it had become. Then: movement. A soft yellow feather, small and floating, came down out of the sky and landed at my muddy feet. A gift from the birds.

The Moonlight Chronicles 2.20.1992

That first summer Lynne and the kids came for several weeks and we all got to experience the joys of camping out along the "singing" river and sleeping in the "cloth cathedral." We quickly learned to close the smoke flaps that usually lay wide open if we were leaving for the afternoon, lest a rain cloud pass by. In the back of my mind I prayed that this new simple way of living might bring my family back together again. I thought that maybe Lynne would agree to live in a yurt if not the tipi. But it wasn't to be, and at the beginning of the new school year, off they drove, the kids' tiny hands waving semi-circles through the back window of the car. I think it was the saddest thing I've ever seen. I crawled back into my lonely tipi and began to write.

Foggy. Awoke at 8 AM. Built wooden hay bin under big fir tree. Mowed. The sky is dark pink and blue. Bob Dylan plays through the headphones. Mowed around pond. Need more grass seed. In looking around, I see it has been a productive year. A lot has been accomplished here at this sacred and treasured place on the river. I am happy now. I am so lucky. My family loves me. The flowers are still blooming. The grass is so green. The air knows of the coming winter.
9.9.1991

I want to live again. I feel the inspirations
coming back. I will be the writer of good words.
The drawer of simple sketches.
The thinker of high thoughts.

The morning cloud cover is beginning to
break up now, with small blue patches showing over Joseph Mountain. The river roars
on, never to stop. The birds sing of the
coming new day. Mr. Owl keeps his solitary
post. Yellow jackets buzz round and round
their papery home in the prairie grass.
Large rocks sit quietly. Home.

BEE

1x

(actual size)

Rode bike around the lake today. The air is warm uptown but drops at
least 5 degrees when I come down here to the river. Down here at
the tipi it will be quite cold this winter. But it will be protected
from the winds. Tonight before retiring to the comfort of my bed
and the company of my books, I cut some of the tall grass by
the front gate. Scattered it along the trail where the dirt is
beginning to show. The tipi smells wet. A damp night coming.

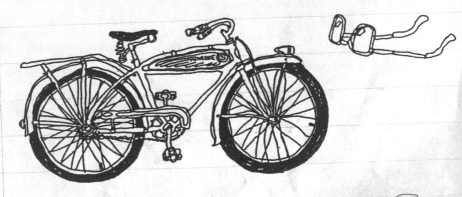

I miss my family. I am still broke and just barely here. Books are saving my soul. I just missed out on 30 days of Shane and Shilo's lives. What am I doing? I feel so small. It's cold and time to get some form of heat in this tipi. Stomping around outside a minute ago I was thinking that I really want to read a book about someone who is trying to do what I am doing. Aren't there others? Where are the river people, the hobos? The ones who have chosen different paths and simpler lives. I want to read about people who live in tipis and how they do it. I want to talk to them. Become their friend. Where are they? I feel so alone. A pioneer in a world made of money. My feet are wrapped in the down bag and with one gloved hand I begin the next Henry Miller book.

There isn't any reason why a person can't still live in a tipi. Close to nature, drying foods, catching wild game. I think that would be a good life. I think to a certain extent, that is how I will live. I must tell Lynne this. I don't expect her to accept my weird ways or join me. But I have to do this. I can no longer live the life of a modern man. Those Indians, they were the wise ones. They knew all about the earth.

Blue sky day. No breeze. Mt. Joseph sits under a blank canvas of blue waiting for Mother Nature to paint the heavens with her clouds. I miss my family. There is a hole in my chest where they are supposed to be. The work of a lifetime awaits.

As fall slowly turned to winter I purchased a propane heater with my meager funds and kept the tipi at a comfortable 60 degrees. After reading, I'd shut it off and leap into bed and lie still as could be, all wrapped up in that down bag with only a small mummy hole for my nose and eyes, and peer up at the stars. In the morning I'd stretch a cold bare arm out of the downy nest and light the heater again with a stick match.

As is the norm in small towns, it wasn't long before most people knew about the guy who had erected a tipi in the meadow. Most just shuddered when I told them I was going to spend the winter sleeping in it. This area experiences very long and very cold winters with

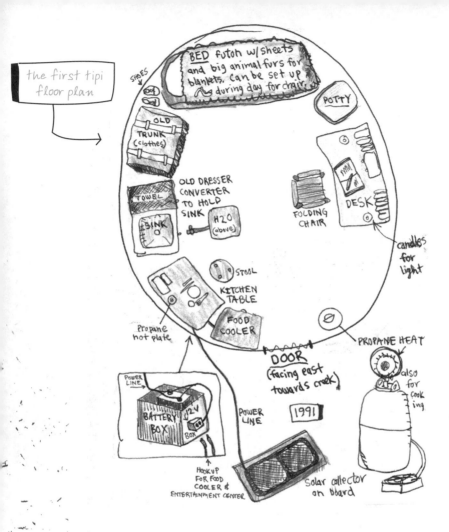

the first tipi floor plan

BED futon w/ sheets and big animal furs for blankets. Can be set up during day for chair.

SHOES

POTTY

OLD TRUNK (clothes)

OLD DRESSER CONVERTER TO HOLD SINK

TOWEL

SINK

H2O (above)

FOLDING CHAIR

DESK

candles for light

STOOL

KITCHEN TABLE

Propane hot plate

FOOD COOLER

DOOR (facing east towards creek)

PROPANE HEAT

also for cooking

POWER LINE

BATTERY BOX

12V BOX

POWER LINE

1991

HOOK UP FOR FOOD COOLER & ENTERTAINMENT CENTER

Solar collector on board

temperatures occasionally dipping below zero. But I hadn't grown a beard or started to wear mountain man leathers, so the townspeople probably figured I was just some young guy who wanted to test himself out.

Right across the property line from the meadow stood an old rickety barn that was filled with rough sawn pine boards owned by an older lady up on the hill. I'd gotten to know her and kept an eye on her house while she wintered down south. She said I could use some of the boards for building projects. After reading the book *Humanure* by Joseph C. Jenkins, I

hastily erected a 4x4 outhouse that didn't cover some
nasty, stinky, dark hole, but utilized a composting sawdust-
filled bucket. With a ready supply of ashes, sawdust, and leafy
material, my own waste was now being composted right along
with all the other biodegradables like apple cores, wilted lettuce, and
grass clippings: a wonderful closed loop-system that had nothing to do
with septic systems or sewage treatment plants. After three years the
fully decomposed and safe material could be used as fertilizer on non-
edible plants.

One of my close neighbors was the town's mayor who tromped
across the bridge and over to the meadow one day to see what I was up
to. He left being concerned about the nearby wetland and that "weird"
outhouse, but all was later okayed by unanimous decision at a city
council meeting.

Later on, I discussed my tipi dwelling idea with the city manager and
he commented that as long as the neighbors weren't complaining or I

wasn't causing an unsightly mess of some kind, the city wouldn't have a problem with it.

At this point the journals become non-existent. I spent that entire cold winter sleeping in the tipi while seeing to my magazine business in the hotel room in town. I even became the manager of those rooms for a while, which was a total disaster as I was kept too busy trying to track down delinquent tenants.

By that next spring I had thought out an entirely new plan: Leave the hotel room and all its modern conveniences behind and move the entire operation over to the meadow! Whether or not I could actually pull this stunt off had yet to be seen, but I knew I was certainly up for the challenge.

summer time
dinner
with friends
→

DOMICILES, DUNGAREES, AND DISCOVERY

"THE NECESSARIES OF LIFE FOR MAN may be distributed under food, clothing, shelter, and fuel; for not till we have secured these are we prepared to entertain the true problems of life with freedom and a prospect of success."

—Henry David Thoreau, *Walden*

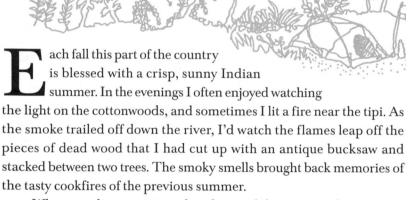

Each fall this part of the country is blessed with a crisp, sunny Indian summer. In the evenings I often enjoyed watching the light on the cottonwoods, and sometimes I lit a fire near the tipi. As the smoke trailed off down the river, I'd watch the flames leap off the pieces of dead wood that I had cut up with an antique bucksaw and stacked between two trees. The smoky smells brought back memories of the tasty cookfires of the previous summer.

When people go camping, they drive or hike to a new place, pop up a tent, and leave all their troubles behind; they enjoy simple meals, a book, and the fact that they aren't looking at the many chores that need to be done around the house.

But what if we could create that feeling of being on a camping trip right in our own homes? Would that even be possible? Certainly that was one of my main goals when coming to the meadow. Eventually it got to the point where if I looked all around, I saw only the beauty and not a bunch of unfinished projects. I also made a pact with myself to start only one project at a time and see it through to completion before starting another.

Carrying a notebook spilling over with new ideas, I visited with the landowners the following spring and tried to explain my latest crazy

← drilled out this hole for hanging on nail on tree. the hole is too small. needs to be bigger.

SHOVEL
*Used for digging post holes and carrying red hot rocks in to the sweating house.

HOE
*have not even used this baby yet. Was bought to dig trenchs for seeds.

*and this is for sure my all time favorite tool. Used to clean out all those dead grasses and hiding sticks that do go poof in a blaze of fire...

*too many tines!

STEEL RAKE

HAMMER HATCHET
*bought for just only 6 dollers at the Trading Post and it is used for all those nail drivings and the sharpenings of many sticks. Also did de bark those tipi poles with it.

ORANGE BUCK SAW
*bought way back in the state of running horses. used to trim limbs, small trees, legs, arms, etc.

CLOSED & OPEN

FOLDING SAW
*a very wicked and mean tool to cut medium logs...

BIG FILE
Used to shear off wood to make it all sm oooooth...

SMALL FILE a tiny half round file used to sharpen the tools with. It is ½ broken off at this end.

OLD TOBACCO KNIFE
*not too much bacer to cut round here but its kept around for sentimental reasons if nothin else.

drawn in the town of PHILOMATH 10:20 PM

NAILS
*and after all those years of scattered nails, now they are all sizes in their proper topperware container. An idea that came to me in one those dreams... 103

ROPE
*one only scraggly little piece that I'll use for some thing some day

TOOL BOX
*made from one old board found in the winter stream bed. It has ② tiny hinges on the other side...

BIG BUCKSAW

~ 6.12.91 ~

US

6.13.9 Today Lynne, and Shane drove all over this town to look for throw rugs for the tipi. We went to a used store called Black beards and got a whole set of silver ware. A soapy brillo pad was used to make them all shiny.

1847 ROGERS BROS. WARRANTED 16 DWT.

PANAMA

idea: to dig a 3-foot-deep circle in the
meadow, line the edges with rock, and
place a new, larger tipi over the top. Their
response was an encouraging "You just do whatever you want there,
Dan." So the next day I grabbed a pick and shovel and spent the next
week carving out the boulder-filled spot. But when it came time to
begin mixing mortar to build the circular wall I just couldn't do it. For
some reason I wasn't able to pour any concrete on what I considered
such a sacred site. Instead I revamped my plan, ordered a new,
stronger tipi, and focused on building a round wooden floor and
installing underground electricity.

If I was indeed going to leave that hotel room behind for good, I
needed to have power to run my small copy machine, which had
become an integral part of creating the photo magazine. After some
discussions with both the county and the city, I secured a
building permit for a tool shed that allowed me to install
electricity. Soon the power company connected a 120-volt
line to a pole I had put up. I dug a trench, buried several
hundred feet of underground cable, and within days
had lights and sound in the tipi! This new development
irked some of my friends who joked that I was selling
out, but solar power was still too expensive and I wasn't
averse to taking full advantage of modern technology
just so long as it didn't restrict my freedom.

My 6-year-old son Shane came for several weeks during spring
vacation and helped me saw boards for the new floor by standing on
the ends. I designed the floor so that it wasn't simply a big ugly plat-
form that the tipi sat on; instead, it tucked up under the edge of the
canvas cover, hidden from view. I ordered a brand new tipi and interior liner. We sat in the room awaiting their arrival and watching the
rains come and go.

I visited with the landowners the following spring and tried to explain my latest crazy idea: to dig a 3-foot-deep circle in the meadow, line the edges with rock, and place a new, larger tipi over the top. Their response was an encouraging "YOU JUST DO WHATEVER YOU WANT THERE, DAN."

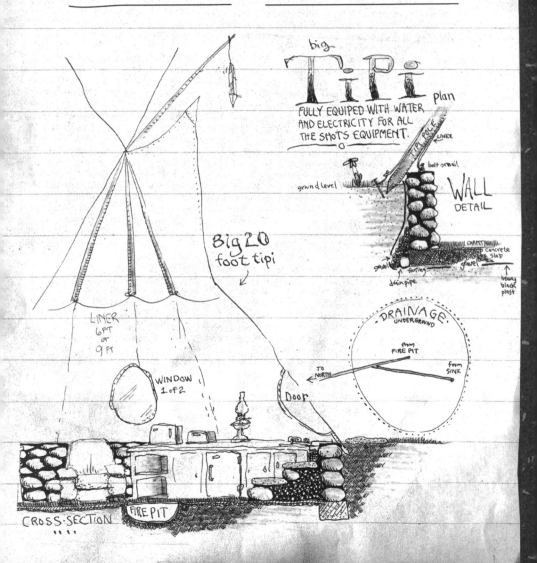

big TiPi
plan

FULLY EQUIPED WITH WATER AND ELECTRICITY FOR ALL THE SHOTS EQUIPMENT.

TIPI POLE
LINER

bolt or nail

ground level

WALL DETAIL

CARPET
concrete slab
gravel
heavy black plast

gravel
footing
drain pipe

Big 20 foot tipi

LINER
6 FT
or
9 FT

WINDOW
1 of 2

DRAINAGE
UNDERGROUND

from FIRE PIT

from SINK

TO NORTH

Door

CROSS-SECTION

FIRE PIT

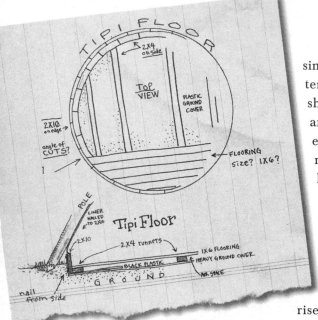

TIPI FLOOR

TOP VIEW

↖ 2X4 on side

PLASTIC GROUND COVER

2X10 on edge →

angle of CUTS?

← FLOORING size? 1X6?

POLE

LINER NAILED TO 2X10

2X10

Tipi Floor

2X4 runners

1X6 FLOORING

HEAVY GROUND COVER

BLACK PLASTIC

AIR SPACE

GROUND

nail from side

In my reading about simple living, I had encountered the idea that you should spend a good amount of time, even several seasons, living on a newly purchased piece of land before bringing in the backhoes and bulldozers. That way you are able to learn all the unique aspects of that particular spot on the earth: where the sun rises; where the wind comes

My plans for the new tipi would allow me to be totally self-sufficient, and free from the flophouse motel room I was still renting to print SHOTS.

from; how the animals move through it; where the most sheltered areas are. By putting up a tent or similar temporary structure and spending time on the land before creating permanent foundations, you quite possibly could avoid placing the house or barn in the wrong spot. There are many moods that move over an area of land, subtle ambiences that need to be respected, or your time spent there will never be all that it could possibly be.

WoodStove

Through all the years I have spent in this one particular meadow, refining and changing the living spaces over and over again, I feel that I have finally been able to discover what the land wants to have on it.

gon fishen

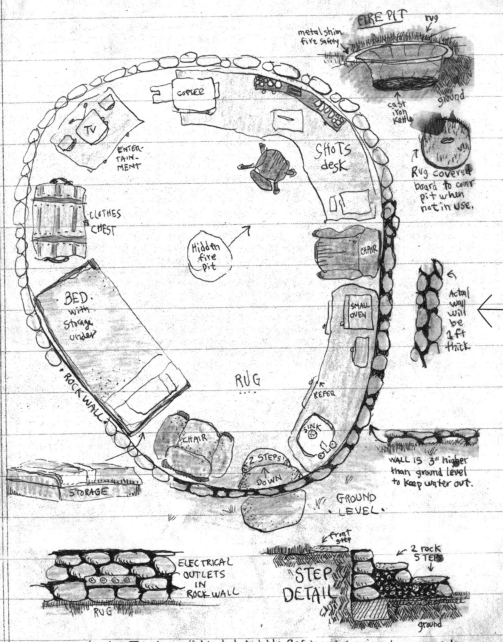

FIRE PIT

metal shim fire safety

rug

cast iron kettle

ground

Rug covered board to cover pit when not in use.

COPIEE

TV

ENTER-TAIN-MENT

CLOTHES CHEST

SHOTS desk

Hidden fire pit

CHAIR

Actual wall will be 1 ft thick

BED. with Storage under

SMALL OVEN

ROCK WALL

RUG

REFER

WALL IS 3" higher than ground level to keep water out.

STORAGE

CHAIR

SINK

2 STEPS DOWN

GROUND LEVEL

ELECTRICAL OUTLETS IN ROCK WALL

RUG

Front step

2 rock STEPS

"STEP DETAIL"

ground

Tankless water heater, T.V. stereo, light at shots table, Refrigerator, copier, typer, computer, propane heater used in washhouse.

Through all the years I have spent in this one particular meadow, refining and changing the living spaces over and over again, I feel that I have finally been able to discover what the land wants to have on it. I have come to literally touch nearly every rock, tree, bush, and object on the 2 acres. All my moving about of stones, trimming of trees, and working the ground has created an incredibly strong bond with the area. It now feels like my very best friend. I get sad and miss it when I am away. When traveling, I envision the big grandfather fir tree and try to tell it I will soon return. When sitting by the river during a sweat, I try hard to listen to all the voices of mankind in its rumblings just as Siddhartha did.

One of my longtime idols and mentors was the New York-based photographer and journalmaker Peter Beard. I had collected every story I could find about him and his famous Hog Ranch in Kenya, a compound of large walled tents, finely furnished but sparingly supplied. He seemed to have the ideal life, coming to the States when business called, then returning to his retreat to create more of his amazingly elaborate handmade journals.

my final blueprint for the tipi interior, complete with electricity!

In keeping with Beard's example, I installed a soft rug in the new tipi, along with an antique oak desk and chair. Shane and I then built a driftwood table to cook on and I found a copper pan and beehive-shaped teakettle. At this point I could have gone way more primitive, but it was early in the game and I had yet to truly let go of a lot of my modern habits and desires.

The last thing that I brought down from town was my small TV/VCR player. I had become hooked on the local PBS station's educational programs, so Shane and I installed an old antenna up in the fir tree one windy day and settled in to enjoy his favorite show, *Star Trek*.

Eventually that PBS station heard about the nutcase who had a TV in a tipi and came over to do a short promo piece that ended up running again and again. I then had to endure my friends' comments, such as "Hey Dan, we saw you on TV last night. *Again!*"

So it was a done deal. On the way out of the room for the last time I visited a nearby dumpster and offloaded all unnecessaries. And during every move thereafter, I did the same. I was learning that if I didn't pay attention and pack out at least as much stuff as I packed in, my space would become filled with all kinds of crap. This has proved to be something that I've had to be almost fanatically diligent about, especially when inhabiting such tiny places.

The new tipi was fantastic. It was very watertight and filled with an unearthly glow during the day and mysterious phosphorescence during a full moon. Lynne and the kids returned for another summer and we planted flowers, rafted the river, swam in the lake, and kept a new bunny in a handbuilt hutch down in the sunken garden. The huge pit I had slaved away to dig months before became a rocky garden that we stepped down into.

AND I CONTINUED TO WRITE:

Maybe the reason all this thinking and figuring about a lifestyle is so heavy on my mind is that I'm in the process of creating a new way to live here at the end of the 20th century. When you look around there are only a few different ways that man lives on the earth. Most drive around a lot. Go shopping. Watch TV And head down busy freeways to work. I guess I'd like to be more like a modern-day hobbit, walking all the slow back roads in big baggy jeans, barefoot and wearing a heavy hooded sweatshirt. On my back would be an ultra-simple pack of stuff that kept the rain off and me warm. I really think this freedom-in-America lifestyle is possible and that's what I want to prove. That's why I have to work so hard to get through all this stuff. I feel that not only can it be accomplished but that it can be an extremely enriching and fulfilling way in which to live.

I know what you're thinking. Sure, this guy chose to simplify his life to the max, but what about showers? How does he stay clean? Ah yes, now I get to explain one of the more fascinating aspects of the Nez Perce culture. Not that I had it in my mind at all to become some kind of neo-Indian or anything. It's just that some of their ideas were so perfect I had to figure out a way to integrate them into my new way of living.

I remember that when I was a wee munchkin, my father took us boys into the neighbors' Finnish sauna. And when I lived in Ketchum, Idaho in the late 70s I used to ride my bike up to the Sun Valley Lodge and walk right in the front door as if I was staying there, go back to the swimming pool area, grab a towel from the smiling attendant, and hop in the sauna. There was something really special and wonderful about sitting in all that heat. It seemed to melt my troubles away.

sweat lodge number two

The Nez Perce people call their sweat lodges The Old Man. Horace Axtell, a Nez Perce elder, says, "We went there for The Old Man.

OVER THE YEARS I've rebuilt and improved my sweat lodge many times. This one is number four.

The One Who Was Wise. We were there to be with him, to get wisdom from him."

One of my friends was a potter who had a sweat lodge. From time to time, he invited me to partake and we would talk of the old ways. Through our discussions we came up with a new way to heat the rocks. Traditionally, a huge fire is built and the rocks are placed in the flames until they are red hot, then transported into the lodge. As you pour cold water on them, the domed space fills with an intense heat. Because I didn't have an overabundance of wood to burn in the meadow, I devised a way to heat the rocks with a propane burner while leaving them in the pit. After several years of experimentation, we have pretty much perfected the method. Since then many of our acquaintances have also built propane-equipped lodges in the area, but they can be very dangerous and I do not recommend constructing one.

So for the first five years or so I was staying clean in a kind of combination Japanese/Nez Perce bathing style. While the rocks were being superheated by the propane burner under them, a dangling metal bucket over the flames heated several gallons of river water to near-boiling.

After the sweat, I'd cool off in the river, then go back to the lodge for a sit-down scrub with the hot water and biodegradable soap.

It was remarkable how much cleaner I always felt compared to taking a conventional shower! It was a deep stimulating kind of cleaning that not only removed the thin outer layer of dirt and dead skin, but purged all the deep toxins that had accumulated as well. And since I started following this regimen, I rarely if ever get a cold or the flu.

The other nice thing about the sauna is that instead of rushing into a chlorinated shower and hurrying to get out because either someone is waiting their turn or you are conscious of using too much water, you just sit back and relax. Some sessions can last as long as two hours if you and

the current sweat lodge

a good buddy are in there and you get to talking. And when you're alone it becomes your "do nothing" time to mull over the day's happenings and to listen to what all those ancient rocks are trying to teach you. I swear that when I take a problem of any kind in to The Old Man, just lay myself entirely open, and not ask for or demand an answer, an answer always emerges. Some of my best ideas were born in those sweats.

The heat is so humbling, reminding me of what is truly important and what is trivial.

I've been hanging out in those attitude adjusters for 14 years now and I still get excited at the prospect of climbing in again.

My skin is still bristling from a sweat taken just after dark. The fire roared. The river up and running hard. The candle went out early, leaving me to think and wonder in the darkness. After going into the icy cold river for the third time the feelings start to come. They are the feelings of your body melting into the earth. Of total relaxation. You are at peace and just floating along when you walk. There is no gravity.
THE MOONLIGHT CHRONICLES 2.8.1992

It may well have been the best summer of our lives. Because my only job was working on the photo magazine in the mornings, I'd take entire afternoons off to hike and play with the kids. We'd go to the lake and build stick forts, or hunt for arrowheads on the shore.

Once again I proposed that we should all live together as "the roving nomads," saying I'd buy some land, provide running water, etc. To be the family that took a vow of "voluntary poverty" in order to live free and have days filled with adventure. But then just like clockwork they piled all their stuff in that darn car and once again I was left standing on the side

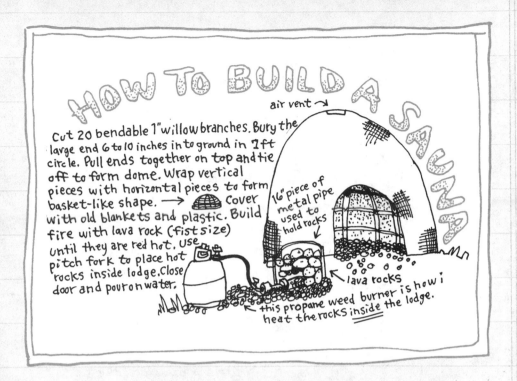

HOW TO BUILD A SAUNA

air vent

Cut 20 bendable 1" willow branches. Bury the large end 6 to 10 inches into ground in 7 ft circle. Pull ends together on top and tie off to form dome. Wrap vertical pieces with horizontal pieces to form basket-like shape. → Cover with old blankets and plastic. Build fire with lava rock (fist size) until they are red hot. Use pitch fork to place hot rocks inside lodge. Close door and pour on water.

16" piece of metal pipe used to hold rocks

lava rocks

this propane weed burner is how i heat the rocks inside the lodge.

of the road crying big sobbing tears as they drove away. It hurt deeply not to be able to share my love of minimalism with the people I cared the most about. In the end, though, I felt I could only suggest and not demand that my kids be raised in a more primitive manner. To ease the pain I continued to write and draw in my newfound magazine called *The Moonlight Chronicles* and started calling myself a Hobo.

HOBOISMS: Of course the obvious first thing you need to do is get rid of all your crap! Garbage cans work well for this task, as do dumpsters. And whoever said you could have all those 29 pairs of shoes ought to be spanked! One or two pairs are plenty! Simple boots and hightop Converse rule! Actually, in our gear-oriented society you must become adept at packing out as much stuff as you're packing in. Plus we all take too many damn pictures, then don't know what to do with them all. We confound then confuse our already too busy lives with all sorts of cheap gadgets that don't even work half the time. Sinks are nasty things that clog up and enable you to let too many dirty dishes pile up in them. Hobos have only one plate, one spoon, and one fork. Visitors be damned! I think what we really need to do is totally abolish "domesticity!" That's right. I say smash all those stupid dishwashers. Blow up the houses. Burn the furniture. Grind up the rugs and everybody has to live in tents and tipis. No running water. No electricity. No phones. Not even any floors. Like the old Indians say, you just sit there in the dirt, man, right there with nothing between you and Mother Nature...

THE MOONLIGHT CHRONICLES 9.10.92

Shane and Shilo playing "elephant"

MORE HOBO THOUGHTS: So there you are. You've learned to live on the edge of society. It doesn't cost too much, maybe just a few thousand a year which you can pick up doing some odd jobs for a few months. But then you just go off and live in a tent somewhere. Out in the bushes. On the edge. Hidden from all those busy folks. And you read lots and think some and get going real slow. 'Cause you've also discovered the most important thing in this lifetime. And it wasn't too easy to figure out. In fact you had to practically die and be reborn again to make that elemental discovery ... that a person really should be able to spend their lifetime learning to praise and appreciate all those things that we encounter. To never be in such a hurry that we don't feel the sun's heat or watch ants crossing a road. That all our eyes perceive is to be studied, honored, and captured in some way for future appreciation. And that's where the Hobo part comes in. Ya gotta live free to be able to do all these things. You can't have phones and schedules and mega stuff to take care of...

THE MOONLIGHT CHRONICLES
9.15.1992

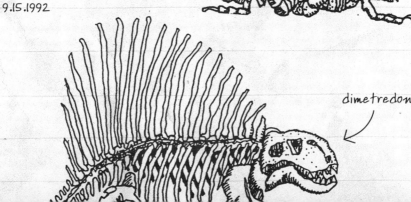

dimetredon

TIPIS, TENTS, AND TRAVEL

"THE LAKOTA WAS A TRUE NATURIST-A LOVER OF NATURE. He loved the earth and all things of the earth, the attachment growing with age. The old people came literally to love the soil and they sat or reclined on the ground with the feeling of being close to a mothering power. It was good for the skin to touch the earth and the old people liked to remove their moccasins and walk with bare feet on the sacred earth. Their tipis were built upon the earth and their altars were made of earth. The birds that flew in the air came to rest upon the earth and it was the final abiding place of all things that lived and grew. The soil was soothing, strengthening, cleansing and healing. That is why the old Indian still sits upon the earth instead of propping himself up and away from its life-giving forces. For him to sit or lie upon the ground is to be able to think more deeply and to feel more keenly. He can see more clearly into the mysteries of life and come closer in kinship to other lives about him..."

—Chief Luther Standing Bear

T hose wonderfully long and lazy tipi days continued on through two more seasons. The winters were especially challenging when I had to run to the river, chop a hole in the ice and run back to the tipi with a bucket of water for the day's supply. I had put up a canvas ceiling and stuffed straw all around the lower edges to keep the cold out. After each snowstorm I'd step outside and sweep the cover clean, then shovel it away from the bottom to eliminate ice buildup. Snowshoes and cross-country skis stood against the tipi wall and were used to explore up river nearly every day. Living in the round space felt totally natural by then, so much so that when I'd go down to be with the family, all those square corners felt kind of creepy.

I had achieved success in a few other experiments by this time. A pen company called Sakura—whose pens I had been using for several years—agreed to send a lifetime supply of them if I mentioned their use in each issue of my ongoing journal, the *Moonlight Chronicles*. While doing a weeklong walk through the wilds of Hell's Canyon, I dreamed up the idea. Back home I made a phone call that secured the deal.

The magazine business had always created lots of scrap paper, but now that I was in the meadow full time there was no nearby dumpster or even a garbage can. So I got a 50-gallon oil drum, cut some triangular

another big winter storm

slots near the bottom and began burning all the papers. When the barrel got one-half full I'd spread the ashes over the meadow grass by tossing several shovel-fulls skyward. That way another closed circle system was created that nurtured the soil and eliminated the need to haul something away. By keeping the barrel covered diligently, rain never made a soggy mess that made the next burning difficult. I also would burn the papers the way I would as a child, either one piece at a time or the whole mess at once, making sure to stir it up as it burned completely. Sometimes I'd watch to see how high the ashes floated into the air. On cold days I'd warm my fingers over the flame. In the end, the task of burning the papers became not just another boring task, but an interesting experience.

thanks to Sakura I have a lifetime supply of these puppies

MICRON03

That next fall I began to feel the need for change once again and I was grow-ing tired of all the people who were visiting out of the blue, sometimes complete strangers who had heard of the guy living in a tipi with all the beautiful flowers. I was re-reading some books by an old Kentucky her-mit/artist named Harlan Hubbard who was also inundated with an over abundance of curious folks. Because of these factors I decided one day to completely

75

HOW TO MAKE A BURN BARREL

1. Get a fifty gallon, steel oil drum.
2. Cut one end out w/chisel.
3. Cut air slots all around the bottom and center with axe or torch.
4. Place barrel on bricks to keep bottom from rotting.
5. Build a wooden top to keep barrel dry when not in use.
6. Stir paper while burning to create clean ashes.
7. ONLY BURN PAPER! NO PLASTIC, GLOSSY MAGS OR STYROFOAM. THEY ARE ALL VERY TOXIC!

CLIP AND SAVE!

change my ways there by the river.

The new vision I had was to build a secret hideaway. You'd only see a narrow trail through the meadow that led to a humble abode hidden in the tall grass. No lawn or flowers. And hopefully not too many visitors. And as with all new visions, I didn't hesitate to act. That very next morning I began dismantling the fancy round flower beds, spreading the rich soil we had hauled in on the surrounding ground. Then I filled in the sunken garden, which took several days. And I vowed to quit mowing all the area that had been manicured like a golf course, to let all the natural grass and weeds return.

Several weeks were spent slaving away at the drawing table as I tried with all my might to envision a new shelter. As much as I loved the tipi I now thought it was too big, too noticeable and too conventional. I went back to studying books like, Native American Architecture by Nabokov and Easton. The underground kivas of the Anastasi were my favorites but I hesitated about digging more holes. Wickiups, wigwams and earth lodges were all considered.

Then while visiting the family in western Oregon I took a camera to several communes I'd heard about and got shots of all the alternative shacks and shanties I could find. One unique looking canvas dome really caught my eye. It had been constructed with a light weight metal framework that from the inside was pretty ugly. But it had a wonderfully large plastic window that stretched across the front and a nifty Velcro door.

I was hoping I could come up with a more natural looking dome.

On the way home I was practically banging my head against the car window, trying to come up with a less expensive and more natural looking dome than the one I'd just seen. By the time the Falcon rolled to a stop in Joseph a whole new idea had become crystal clear. I'd build the next shelter just like all those domed sweat lodges I'd been erecting, only larger and with a wooden floor!

It may not seem like much, but to me it was a huge revelation. Those big advances in further simplifying what was already pretty darn basic in most people's eyes filled me with a great sense of elation. Why spend $1200 (that I didn't have) on some heavy metal framework when what I really wanted was a much smaller dome made entirely of natural materials?

That next day I was on the phone selling the tipi to a friend who had expressed an interest and I began clearing a spot for the new hut, closer to the river and hidden behind some bushes. I gathered several armloads of bright red dogwood branches from the river's edge and cleaned all the small branches off. Then I constructed a 9 X 12 egg-shaped floor that had an electrical line under it. I then drilled large holes all around the perimeter of the floor, stuck the large end of the dogwood limbs in and started pulling each one to the center where they were all tied together to form a basket-like shape.

my dome, made entirely from natural materials!

large over-lapped door

port holes

It wasn't long before I realized I was busy creating an even smaller space than the tipi, but believe it or not I was looking forward to the upcoming challenge of having to get rid of even more extraneous items. I would have to let go of the fancy oak table and chair, put my clothes into a

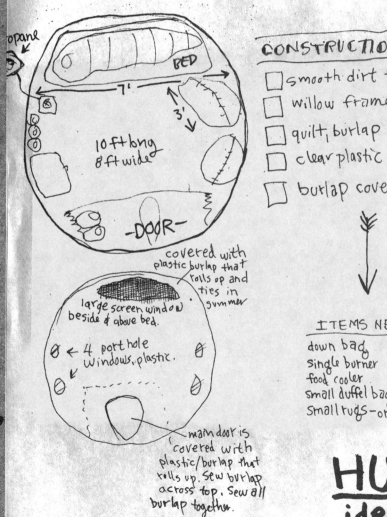

11.28

CONSTRUCTION PLAN

- ☐ smooth dirt floor (plastic-pad small carpets)
- ☐ willow frame work (no tie)
- ☐ quilt, burlap interior
- ☐ clear plastic vapor barrier
- ☐ burlap cover stapled

propane

BED

7'

3'

10 ft long
8 ft wide

-DOOR-

covered with
plastic burlap that
rolls up and
ties in
summer

large screen window
beside & above bed.

← 4 port hole
windows, plastic.

main door is
covered with
plastic/burlap that
rolls up. Sew burlap
across top. Sew all
burlap together.

ITEMS NEEDED

down bag
single burner
food cooler
small duffel bag
small rugs—or use brown rug

HUT
ideas

79

LIGHT SOURCES

DOOR

Hang stuff from willow on walls.

2 jars pens
tape
stamps
ink
TP
H2o
Dict.
bugs

new size window

PACIFIC DOMES

lists
calen.

small basket hung for pens

and about

That friend showed up
and we took down the tipi
and away he went.
I didn't even shed a tear.

ELL

low!

at ted's.

1. fo
2. c
3. sell big desk & chair
4. buy coffee table & stool like Lynnes. (extra stu-
   in alternati
   containers)

large chest of drawers to accom-odate business stuff.

copier up.

to keep table clear. NO light on table. G antique hanging with fringed shad

TV

table

garbage

food box
*rest of food in jars

Ref.

file boxes

PEN

per ides on futon

WATER SYSTEM?

drawers

low table and stool

Box for stamps

kitchen in front of window. hang pots from ceiling.

*move around table!

THE Hut

MORE IDEAS

WORK

Store

rocks around base

folding chair

small duffel bag, and somehow lose the two top drawers of the already short dresser.

Soon the new structure was wrapped up and completed. I rolled the largest rocks I could find near the front door area. That friend showed up and we took down the tipi and away he went. I didn't even shed a tear. I was just too excited about the hut to even think about the tipi being gone. And what was left of my meager possessions soon found their place in the new home. In that incredibly cozy space you could lay on the floor and look up at the round framework of Dogwood. Laying snuggly on top of the frame were several old colorful quilts and blankets which you could also see. Next came several layers of heavy water-proofing plastic, then a layer of thin

THE NEW HUT

INTERIOR

foil insulation. The outer skin consisted of wide burlap strips purchased from a farm supply store and sewn together with a big needle and thin hemp string. There were two round windows covered with clear boat vinyl, a heavy wool blanket for the door and the thick pad and carpet from the tipi, trimmed down to fit the smaller floor.

This new mini home was very different than the tipi. You still had to duck down through a small doorway as before, but once inside everything had to be done in a sitting position because the ceiling was only 5 feet above. I could stand in the very center only if I cocked

my head to the side, which I did each morning when I got dressed. As I laid back on the bed roll/seat I could see the bright light streaming in from the large window at my back. It was a perfect place to read and draw. I could cook up my favorite stir fry meals on a 2-burner propane stove top that sat on the floor to the left. I could listen to the radio or watch the tiny TV which were both situated just to the right of the doorway. I could make all the copies I wanted while working on a new magazine from the small Canon copy machine that sat on top of the dresser which had been sawed off so that it only had two drawers remaining. And instead of that big old desk I used a 2 X 2 chunk of masonite board as a lap table. A few nights prior, during a brainstorming session, I had thought of that idea and the next day burnt the desk and chair in celebration!

Whenever there was a moon of any consequence, I found it hard to close my eyes at the end of a hard day. I'd watch it as it came through the window, making a spot on the floor that slowly moved. There was also a string of tiny Christmas lights strung all about the ceiling that illuminated the many colored quilts. This created another sight I couldn't seem to take my eyes off. I guess I was just totally amazed that I had been able to build such an absolutely cool tiny home that kept me warm and feeling secure, and all for only $75!!

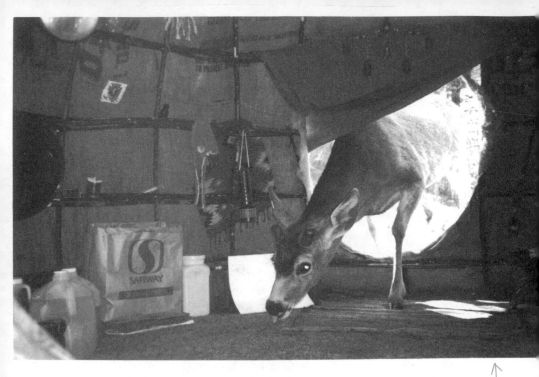

For the next two years I became more secretive, still feeling the strain of too many visitors during the tipi days. In the hut I felt like a true hobo down there by the river. The local deer population became extremely friendly. One even stepped a foot INSIDE the hut as I was feeding him little carrots.

Because the door was unlockable, I did have to deal with the occasional marauding teenager looking for a few thrills. When I was away they would sometimes come inside and mess around with the copier and other things.

For the following two years this lifestyle went on as the meadow slowly closed in around the hut. I built another improved sweat lodge and continued to write my yearly letter to the landowners about any new areas I might have cleaned up and restored. At some point I raised my own rent to $200/year thinking that would at least cover their yearly tax bill on the land. The visitors all but vanished and I spent many days in peace.

Well, for a short while anyway. That ongoing vision of creating an ultimate quiet place where I could awaken at dawn and live in an absolute state of pure bliss never seemed to quite materialize for more than a few days at a time, even after all those years.

Within two months two big changes would come about that would rock my world to the core and change that hermit-like lifestyle for years.

I had been hankering to rid myself of the gas guzzler that sat up on the hill, honking at me to go on a road trip whenever I felt like relaxing. On the next trip down to see the kids I hung a "For Sale" sign in the window and a week later found myself car-less and 350 miles from home. After the

suddenly I was carless and 350 miles from home

visit I avoided the expensive bus fare, threw a pack on my back and began a long walk home, across the many varied landscapes of Oregon.

Before leaving on that rainy day in March I had spotted a cool new pair of boots in an *Outside* magazine ad, called the 800 number and asked the owner of the company if he'd mail me a pair for the journey. That one call proved to be a turning point as he not only liked the sound of what I was doing, but sent a pair for free! And several months later, offered me a job as roving-ambassador-who-is-seeking-the-secret-to-life-by-drawing-stuff! The California based Simple Shoe Company agreed to publish my *Chronicle* zine several times a year with their catalog in the back. Many thousands would be printed and sent out across the planet to all their customers. In turn I was paid a handsome salary and told to go draw the world!! I was in shock for months.

fancy new business card

The second thing that happened was that Lynne graduated from college and secured a new job with the Forest Service in a town only 6 miles from the meadow! All of the sudden I felt like a yo-yo. Now the ones I loved were practically at my back door, but this new opportunity had me out and about and back and forth to the shoe headquarters in Santa Barbara for upwards of six months each year for the next 5 years.

My little *Moonlight Chronicles* about the simple life went from around 100 eager subscribers to between 30-50,000 unknown readers and the quiet hobo was instantly flung out into the larger world, photo shows in France, and crisscrossing the continent drawing up a storm.

During one extended stay back home Lynne and I braved the cold weather and enlarged the hut to include an extra room that had a big window facing southward towards the mountain. I continued to hope that the family would decide that the modern day conveniences weren't worth all the hassle and would come stay at my

Skylight

plastic boat vynal. Removable for hot days!

the HUT
add on

1. Add on smaller dome off south side. About the size of the sweat.
2. Use old window as entery way.
3. make long window in new part
4. make ceiling sitting height
5. addition is shorter and smaller.

door

long window

add port hole

Doorway thru old window

add port holes

|← 12 →|← 7 →|

DOOR

seat

Food box becomes supply box and table to do computer work

Shelves of books

copier

food transfered to jars

build curve into new flooring from edge of door frame

FIREPLACE

place more often, but in the end they declined to do so. It was really strange to have cut into the pristine hut to make it bigger and that action caused it to somehow lose its magic. After several months of feeling that I had ruined a perfect shelter I decided to take it all down and once again burnt the remains to clean away old mistakes. Plus with all the traveling I was then experiencing , I didn't want to worry about the place being vandalized.

So came the phase in the meadow when I began to purchase rugged 4-season mountain tents that could be put up when back home then dismantled and thrown in the back of the car for trips. Yes, I was back in a miniature Suzuki Swift during those run around years and had to give up the idea of walking everywhere and saving the planet from all our polluting ways. It was a compromise that I felt was worth it given the amazing experiences that were coming my way and enhancing the *Chronicles*.

THE HUT ADD ON WITH WINDOW

As much as I had admired that sturdy hut, I soon became totally enamored with the even simpler idea of living in tents. Soon I was creating scrapbooks filled with photographs of exotic and expensive expedition tents pitched in the most amazing places. Luckily I had secured yet another sponsor over the years and was given many tents to test and write about by Sierra Designs. Believe it or not I actually liked the smaller space even more and happily gave up all the extra cooking paraphernalia in trade for a diet of fruit, vegetables, and no-cook foods. "Dirty dishes suck!," became my mantra.

I started hanging out with rock climbers, dirt bags, and train hopping hobos of all kinds who dwelt in ragged tents for most of the year. Then for a short, albeit uncomfortable time, I went so far as to have only a bivy bag for shelter, which consists of nothing more that a tough nylon sack that protects your sleeping bag from the elements.

Then one humid night as I lay sweating under the stars on Catalina Island off the coast of southern California, I asked myself, "When will this all stop? When I'm wandering completely naked and alone with absolutely nothing to call my own?"

Shilo at the tent site

In one sense I had really come to an end. I had taken the concept of minimalism for human shelter to its very limits. But only as far as modern day technology was concerned. What I began to envision from that

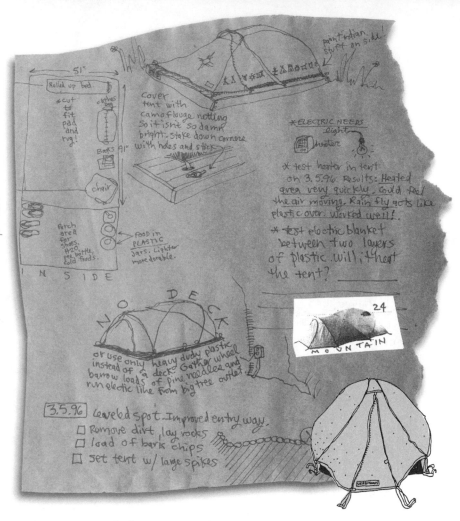

("WHY CAN'T YOU BREAK THE TWO POUND BARRIER?" I would holler over the phone.

point on was a whole new yet undiscovered concept of shelter that was so light and so small that you could literally wad it up and put it in your pocket! Then push a hidden button or pull a small cord and poof! it becomes a little tent to protect you from the bugs and rain!

Unfortunately, not being of scientific mind I had to end my quest, but not before I'd called the tent designers at several major outdoor companies to admonish them for hiding behind their latte cups and reissuing the same basic tent technology year after year. "Why can't you

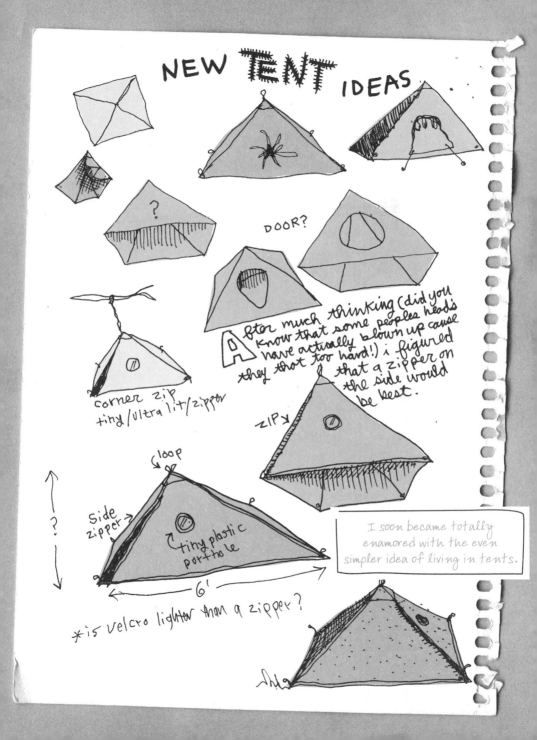

NEW TENT IDEAS

?

DOOR?

corner zip
tiny/ultra lit/zipper

After much thinking (did you know that some peoples heads have actually blown up cause they that too hard!) i figured that a zipper on the side would be best.

ZIP▸

loop

Side zipper▸

tiny plastic porthole

?

6'

*is velcro lighter than a zipper?

I soon became totally enamored with the even simpler idea of living in tents.

break the two pound barrier," I hollered over the phone. They just laughed and said to call back in 20 years. So this tent loving phase lasted for quite some time as I concentrated more on creating drawings and stories than the meadow.

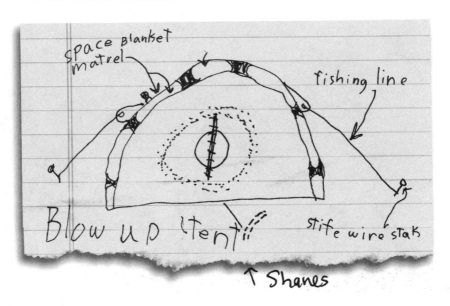

space blanket
matrel

fishing line

Blow up 'tent'''

stife wire stak

↑ Shanes

One of the other experiments that worked out during this period was the creation of an exercise tree. That town that Lynne and the kids had been living in was very athletic oriented. When out walking we'd come across wood chip covered exercise stations. These areas had several posts and beams running this way and that with short pipes jutting out in various places. An instructional panel nearby explained how to stretch, do leg lifts, pushups and other exercises. Back home I picked out one of the larger cottonwood trees and drilled three holes in it on different sides. Then I found a chrome-plated pipe that slid into the holes and I was able to do all the same stretches and exercises . I added

At one point we wanted to make our own tent. Shane even drew his idea too

A 20 BELOW ZERO NIGHT!

a 25 lb. dumb bell and a sit up pad and was able to place all three items in behind the tree when not it use. This was the kind of low impact design I was most interested in. Take a good idea, then boil it down to its essentials, so if you didn't look hard, you proba- bly wouldn't even notice that it was there in the meadow.

The new concept of taking my shelter with me as I traveled around was quite fascinating for me and I pondered it at great length. Once after being on the road for over 30 days, I pulled into company headquarters and reported my findings to the big wig, which was actually a laid-back surfer type who loved to joke

around and drive fast cars. I told him that I'd only spent just over $300 since leaving home and he laughed saying that he spent that much taking all us yahoos out to dinner in Santa Barbara!

The way I was able to travel so far on so little had everything to do with the current tent I was hauling around in the car. Here's a typical day. I'd cruise all day, usually having a vague destination in mind. I'd stop here and there to make sketches and notes then drive on, eating out of a box of food on the floor of the car that contained crackers and cheese, a loaf of fresh sourdough bread, a jar of peanut butter and jelly, some peeled carrots and a few apples found hanging off some wild tree somewhere, plus a jug of fresh water. Every once in awhile I'd zip through a fast food joint to grab a 99 cent burger, then zoom away, eating as the odometer clicked off the endless miles.

ON THE ROAD WITH A NEWER, BIGGER CAR

So. Hike about 3 miles and a half up to the top, then follow ridges to the back side of the island. A steep drop down to the ocean below. Munch carrots. Listen to radio. And think in a pure way. Way up here. All alone. I don't know how it is for you, but some times people rilly freak me out. It's like there's 2 people inside this body. One forces me to move in, up close, to confront people, anyone, even strangers, or strange people. It's a terrifically uncomfortable thing to do. But I've always made myself do it anyway. Back in the newsphotography days I think maybe I was doing it to

about 60°
4 PM
a few clouds

impress the readers. Sort of a "see, i can find the most bizarre person you can imagine, and make their picture," in places most people wouldn't consider going without an armed guard! So maybe I'm still sort of doing that. Trying to act normal and draw just whoever, when rilly my insides are going "run man, get outta here," or "this is _too_ scary, lets book dude." So any time alone is reel frosting on the old cake of life. To me solitude and contemplation feel a lot more natural than sittin around yakking to everybody. Think I'll shut up now......

from the <u>MOONLIGHT CHRONICLES</u>

Come nightfall I'd begin the hunt for a secret place in which to sleep. Any bush or large rock to hide behind would usually suffice. I slept on High School and College football fields, behind old churches, on the edge of State Parks, in the lonely woods, under no camping signs, and on golf courses, which I might add are not the best places as all that manicured greenness stays that way because of sprinklers. Sprinklers that pop up and soak everything in the middle of the night! Including unsuspecting super tramps enjoying the perfect camping spot of a putting green!

I ended up pitching tents on the outskirts of Paris, in the dust of the Haleakala crater in Hawaii, and amongst the sandy boulders on the coast of Baja. What a deal, I thought, wherever you go, your home can come along with you. And in the end, after all those years of experimentation, I still think that tents are the most romantic, meaningful and majestic shelters made by man. There's nothing quite like climbing inside a really high quality tent and riding out a terrific squall. You're there, dry as a bone, while a mere inches away, through that thin layer of space-age material, all hell is breaking lose. I've always thought that any ancient Indian would have given his eye teeth for such an amazing light and durable buffer from the elements.

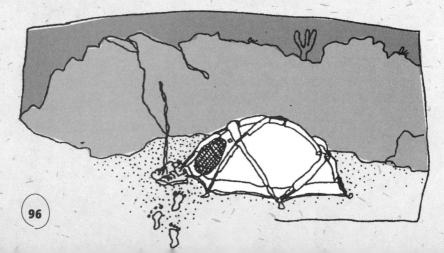

Canoga Park (CA)
818-700-8541
send: color copies
of personal greeting
cards

WE 212-777-0029 Jan Collier- Artist Rep
contact thru Barbara

VINE Kudor
mark odegard
1624 Harmon Pl.
mpls MN 55403
612-338-5090

PIX 400/story 75

Rosehips
edit MC:

FEEL
the
GLORY

CAR rearend trans. leak
drive line boot, alignment
thermostat,

goldfish in pond next
summer
daises from James

Ranch vnt cellar

guest
read In Cold Blood.
see movie too.   signing

Taxes paid 8.22
$1,223.40

Drumming   ice cream truck
I study skippers w/Shane   Book
Desolation Angels
Spokane Book Signing BookFair $
3:15
gather flower seeds at James'
draw cabins at lake
"I MISS MY HAPPINESS"

get book & drum from Pete
book- Bound f/ Glory by W. Guthrie
Arrowhead hunting   grant plum
tree ?
Innaha bike Ride
la Gorda & Base Camp
Snake River Paddle
tree house - Palmer Junction
Eric 437-3702
SPRING - dig up daisys at Munsch

mt. Freak
blve $150
blve -8.99
work
fishtrap

RAW #8 to will Chau   Lynne 1998
AUG 20 1999
send stories on PAC to mom
Send Hells Canyon book to travel mags
call Mary & Mark 503-502-21??
RICE 541-715-6194
ALAZAR - Bill
Sue-8065 TED-3137
CHUCK-46...

MOVIE by Dianeov
The magnificent
obsession of
Everett Ruess

Joanne Zekowsk.   Wynne book

chuck-44656

NUTELLA 800-337-7376
#2212

Journal book press ven 7806

Before long though I was seeing my stash of magazine issues grow and grow with nowhere to put them. Being somewhat road weary I drew up some plans one night for a small wooden beach shack that could be built up under the trees on the hillside. At the age of 40 I felt that I now deserved a more regular abode after living in all those miniature places for so long. I began to wander the lake shore and gather odd pieces of drift wood, hauling them back to the meadow. I leveled out a spot near the outhouse. And soon a whole new idea of lifestyle began to grow way in the back of my mind. It was time to settle down a bit and become more conventional.

HOW BUSY I BECAME!

— OF —
HOBBIT HOLES
— AND —
THIEVES

"IN A HOLE THERE LIVED A HOBBIT. Not a nasty, dirty, wet hole, filled with the ends of worms and an oozy smell, nor yet a dry, bare, sandy hole with nothing in it to sit down on or to eat: it was a hobbit-hole, and that means comfort. It had a perfectly round door like a porthole, painted green, with a shiny yellow brass knob in the exact middle. The door opened on to a tube-shaped hall like a tunnel: a very comfortable tunnel without smoke, with paneled walls, and floors tiled and carpeted, provided with polished chairs, and lots and lots of pegs for hats and coats–the hobbit was fond of visitors. The best rooms were all on the left-handed side (going in), for these were the only ones to have windows, deep-set round windows, looking over his garden, and meadows beyond, sloping down to the river."

–The Hobbit

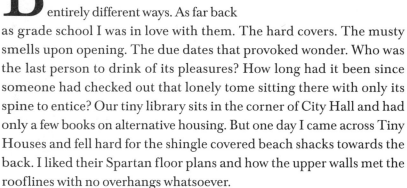

Books are magical things that can entrance a soul to think in entirely different ways. As far back as grade school I was in love with them. The hard covers. The musty smells upon opening. The due dates that provoked wonder. Who was the last person to drink of its pleasures? How long had it been since someone had checked out that lonely tome sitting there with only its spine to entice? Our tiny library sits in the corner of City Hall and had only a few books on alternative housing. But one day I came across Tiny Houses and fell hard for the shingle covered beach shacks towards the back. I liked their Spartan floor plans and how the upper walls met the rooflines with no overhangs whatsoever.

After a few weeks of gathering cast off and left over materials that no one else wanted, I went to work with a hammer and saw and constructed a 6X10 building with a slightly sloping roof. To the west was an old four-pane window that looked down onto the herds of deer that passed through the meadow. The door was made of 2X4's on edge, weighed a ton and was hung on 3 big hinges. Towards the back was a shelf up high for the magazines and below a chest that held all my journals and accumulated paper work. At the window I put another desk and chair that I had found. Within days I'd installed a

THE NEW SHACK

telephone/answering machine, a laptop computer and several cameras that I used for freelance assignments. But an odd feeling was rising in my gut. After spending so much time in round structures, the room felt too boxy, too cold in the corners. The uninsulated walls made it tough to heat. I'd sit there for hours, writing and taking care of the expanding business, but never liked how it felt, even though from the outside it looked very cool. The entire thing was covered in large mossy cedar shakes that a neighbor had given me after they tore down a garage. Like most things in the meadow I made the building appear to have been there for many years. During this time I was spending a lot of time at the kids house

SHACK
plans

roof too
FLAT

10   94
4X8
PLYWOOD
SHACK
PORTABLE!

DOOR

—get tired of livin in some place you can just thrown the damn thing in the back of a pickup and move it to somewheres else! or hook up a tractor and move it to the other end of the property for a new view!

when not on the road. The new building was used as a studio although sometimes I'd stay there after a long day of work and an evening sauna.

That next year I added on a 5 X 6 addition to the back for a better place to sleep and a small counter to cook on. I'd found a beautiful wooden window that cranked open and built it into the back wall. That's when I had the realization that there was indeed somewhat of a method to my madness. Each year all the wonderfully warm months would go sailing by without me having built much of anything, then I'd be seized by huge desires to create something new, just as the cold weather hit! And during the winter of 1998 it happened again.

After spending so much time in round structures, the room felt too cold in the corners.

construction of the underground Kiva behind the studio

My son and I had been hanging out at the studio carving on walking sticks when I got a wild idea to begin digging a big hole into the hillside directly behind the existing back wall. I thought I might be able to enhance that boring space by creating an underground cubby hole for sleeping in that you entered by crawling through a small opening in the back wall.

existing studio

↖ path leads to small doorway

1999
UNDERGROUND KIVA

WINTER 1999

EXTERIOR DOOR

work roof poles into rock work along with flashing

metal stove

several layers of plastic

PLASTIC

TARPAPER

cut door hole nail in frame that extends out beyond wall. Surrounds in mortared from river.

JUN 21 9

lots of room for meditation and sleep.
TOP VIEW
BRICKS

1. burn bottom of board
2. assemble circle using screws
3. apply outer coverings— underground wiring
4. lay stone inside circle.

cut all edges on wall pcs.

poles 4"
2x6
BRICK
pre-drill pole

skilight hole sticks up above
poles
tar paper
plastic

HoBoSTIX are handcarved by Dan and Shane on the sunny banks of the Wallowa River in Eastern Oregon. Walk everyday. Laugh alot. Go FIND your own BLISS.

H•BoSTIX

BOX 109 JOSEPH OR 97846

Shane didn't think much of the idea as he was put to shoveling that very first day, but I went a bit nuts and dug away in that cement-like ground for the next 11 days until I had a good sized circular hole. To keep the snow out I stretched a waterproof tarp between three trees and started to build. At the time I didn't realize the significance of those actions. And how a future milestone was in the making. How that tiny round room would transform everything I had done up to that point. That builder's bliss was indeed, just around the corner.

You see, what happened was this. After finishing up the round room with sweet smelling pine boards I'd gathered up and saved over the years, I connected it via a short passageway to the studio. A skylight was built into the roof and I put on a temporary latch and went on to other things. Then one day I noticed some pine needles and dirt on the bedding and realized someone had come in through the skylight while I was away. I quickly finished it with a strong metal frame and lock and thought I'd solved the problem. Unfortunately some crafty thieves had other ideas.

A few days later I came down off the hill to the studio planning on a late night of work and found the massive wooden door ripped sideways and hanging open! The robbers had simply removed the pins from those large hinges and torn the door open backwards!

THE DOOR THAT WAS TORN OFF

I found the massive wooden door ripped sideways and hanging open! The robbers had simply removed the pins from those large hinges and torn the door open backwards!

After quickly calling the police I found that the intruders had carted off over $5000 worth of cameras, computer equipment, outdoor gear and even some of my clothes! I was stunned and deeply hurt. The two 35mm Leica cameras had been used to shoot all those thousands of photographic images in the 80's. A real tragedy since they didn't even have light meters and couldn't be of value to the average snapshooter. Plus they were very expensive. A Nikon and all its lenses were also taken.

The local cops were unable to recover any of the missing items. I sat back for days wondering what it all meant. Had I gathered together too much crap? Was it some message from above to return to those simpler times? Was this a tough lesson that I could learn from? Wildly wicked scenarios of me catching them in the act clouded my confused mind. Then I acted.

No I didn't start packing a pistol and firing it off at suspects. Without thinking and not knowing where it would all lead I started to pull those wonderful shakes off the building one morning. A fire was started nearby. If I couldn't build a secure studio in the meadow I thought, then I just wouldn't have one at all. For the next 8 days that fire roared as I slowly dismantled and burnt every piece of wood in that stupid studio.

As the fire died down I peered into that narrow passageway that led to the underground room. "Hold on just a minute, " I hollered. " What if I just totally downsized all my stuff and set up shop in the small room!?" Yes, yes, I sang as I danced around in a tiny circle. I thanked the Old Man where the idea more than likely originated,

and I even thanked those damn robbers for unburdening me from things I apparently didn't need. And as in the past I immediately went to work on the new idea.

Finally I felt I was free forever from the tyranny of square buildings!

Some broken cobblestones that I had picked up from a sidewalk project up town were placed in meandering rows to form a patio out front. And a new door was built from the old one that fit over the passageway. An obvious taunting to any future thieves to just go ahead a try to break through this door! With its welded hinge pins!! To complete the rocky wall, large boulders were then rolled around it and set in place with no mortar.

Finally I felt I was free forever from the tyranny of square buildings! Once again I found my hobbit self kneeling down to enter a sacred

The view looking towards the door at the studio. See the raccoons tail?

THE NEW INTERIOR

the finished exterior

round room. And the best part was that this absolutely perfect shelter was stumbled upon by believing in intuition and instinct. Sitting on the hillside looking down at that just violated studio I really had no idea what I was supposed to do. And for the first two days of its burning, I truly didn't know what the next step was going to be. Yet something told me to keep the fire burning.

That room. That miniscule place of peace. That circle filled with heavenly light, is only 8 feet from side to side. The golden pine ceiling is 4 feet off the carpet near the door and rises like a miniature amphitheater on the back side to 5 feet. On the roof lies 2 feet of soil where weeds, wild grasses and deer hang out. Being underground it's a cinch to heat. On hot summer days the room stays at a crisp 58 degrees. That's because the temperature of the ground always stays around 55 degrees. It's why so many animals burrow into it and stay warm in their little fur coats during the winter. Those rabbits and ground squirrels are smarter than we think.

And I've often wondered why, if the Indians who used to inhabit cold regions were smart enough to dig down into the ground and construct pit houses that they then stretched their tipi covers over, why us dumb white people insist on building way up in all that cold air, then struggle to keep things heated? Instead of using the earth as a natural heat source, we keep creating more highly insulated and tighter and tighter houses that actually make new home owners sick for months from all the toxins being released. Do we even know what fresh air feels and smells like blowing through an open window any more?

On hot summer days the room stays at a crisp 58 degrees.

Over the years since building the room only one problem has arisen. Or I guess it sort of marched in. Carpenter ants! Who my buddy says "can smell that sweet pine wood a mile away." You know the type. Large black troopers who love nothing better than to chew a perfectly good board to dust like some demented out of control sanding machine. Fortunately , through the graces of our wonderful modern day science, I am able to combat the intruders by simply placing several ant traps inside and out a couple of times a year. Even though the room was totally waterproofed with multiple layers of plastic and tar paper, they still seemed to fine their way in. Buggers.

For years and years I stayed clean by washing up in the sweat lodge. Nobody seemed to walk large arcs around my being when up town so I figured I must be keeping fairly decent. Lynne had always said that she'd never come live in the meadow with me unless I got a "real shower." So one day I put the old noggin in create mode and thought up a way to have one. A few years earlier I had nailed together some old fence boards to form a 4 X 5 dressing room down near the river.

Because I had dug in underground electricity nearby I ran the cord up the side of the structure and attached a 110 volt water heater element that was set into a 10 gallon plastic bucket up on the roof. A 6-inch piece of pipe with shut off valve was installed through the roof and into the bucket. Then by simply filling the bucket with a few gallons of river water and flipping the switch, I had roiling hot water cascading down my dirty self at the end of a hard day's work! All the soap is biodegradable. A small propane heater nearby makes even winter showering, when ice is on the river, a real joy. It didn't bring Lynne to live in that place of peace but it sure is fun to see her run back and forth from the shower to the sweat lodge in one of my big shirts when she's visiting!

There is an interesting story to tell regarding that primitive shower. A few years ago I rode a three-wheeled racing trike 4500 miles from Oregon to Florida via San Diego. When you pedal between 30 and 100 miles a day, the last thing you want to do is crawl in your dank sleeping bag without a shower. So for all those 100-plus days of the trip I made a point of somehow finding a way to clean up. I snuck into RV Camps, dodged the doormen at college gyms, asked politely

at high school locker rooms, and sometimes made the public restroom at fast food joints my personal bathroom! Expensive motel rooms were out of the question.

Now most modern folks would take one look at my hand-filled, gravity-fed shower and say, "What a pain in the butt! You mean you have to manually fill it? Then wait half an hour before showering? No way!"

But now that I'm back home safe and not begging for showers, I think I must be in heaven. At any time of the night or day I can wander over, fill up the bucket, and in just a few minutes take a hot and invigorating shower! Believe me, I enjoy each and every one. And there seems to be a good lesson here I think. Because I spent all those days struggling to keep clean, I now have a whole new appreciation for the ultra simple shower I now have. Plus I'm not wasting energy keeping a huge tank of water hot for times when I'm not even around like modern day water heaters do. Much like the Zen teachings of "pack wood, carry water," I enjoy every minute of each shower BECAUSE I had to do some work and WAIT some for the pleasure.

the coast of France

It has been over 4 years now since I had that break-through and decided to go underground and live like the rabbits. In that wondrous room, lit by the bright skylight above and a small jelly jar in the door, the silence is endless. I can unplug the phone and write whole books without distraction of any kind. I can hear the deer and are usually awakened momentarily each night by their pounding hooves as they pass directly over on the path above. In that room I feel altogether safe.

CAMPOUT

Why would I leave this place? It's like the worlds perfect camping spot!

Just like I did as a child in the cupboard. Within that space I can dream the dreams of an innocent child. Ideas can be driven hard to far distant shores, returning in bits and pieces, sometimes whole and finished, sometimes in shreds and need-ing love and attention. Stories appear unasked for near the spot of moonbeam that crosses the floor, and can be plucked up and written down without disturbing their unique voices. It's as if I've found my home of homes. A womb. A place that I sometimes don't want to crawl out of.

In fact it's so nice that I even find it hard to get out camping in the summer these days! As I'm doing all the work of packing and planning for a few nights of being away in the woods, I keep looking out at the hammock in the aspens, the distant river through the weave of trees and blurt out, "Why am I leaving this place?" It's like the world's perfect camping spot! There's a shower, lettuce pushing up in the garden, comfortable chairs, a sauna, books, privacy... "Why go?"

These are the kinds of powerful thoughts that leave me thinking it will truly be a gift to grow old here on this small acreage. Surely I will get to travel more in the near future. Crossing my fingers. And I plan on camping lots in the surrounding hills, just breaking away for whole weekends for raucous walk-abouts. But as the salad days roll in and my hair slowly greys in a winter wind, I can see an old man sitting under a tree. There to watch the leaves turn or tending quietly to the small garden on the terrace. His life will be a quiet one down there by the river where no one goes. Hurrying will be a thing of the past. He'll laugh at the stars and cry with crows. With a pen in his hand and a pad in his pocket he will record the meadow's changing moods, count fallen leaves, make his work the arranging of thumb-sized rocks down by the dock. And he'll sit with The Old Man in silence, learning to hear the river, just like Siddhartha did 2000 years ago.

LiFE
— IN THE —
MEADOW

"He noticed that the river's voice spoke to him. He learned from it; it educated and taught him. The river seemed like a god to him and for many years he did not know that the very wind, every cloud, bird and beetle is equally divine and knows and can teach just as well as the esteemed river. But when this holy man went off into the woods, he knew everything; he knew more than you and I, without teachers, without books, just because he believed in the river."

—Siddhartha

Now I know why they call it fall. Because during that season everything starts falling. The leaves, needles, cones and apples come twirling and tumbling down from their high summery perches. Dead and dying sticks of various lengths come unhinged from above and find their way to meadow floors. The levels of once fat rivers fall to form twisting, snaking meanders through rocky streambeds. And in October the temperature falls too, from cobalt skies and t-shirts to the first cold rain with snow swirling on the highest peaks, some melting on the warm backs of shaggy mountain goats while others hit the rocky ground in a frozen stasis until spring. Us humans unfold warmer coats and slip on first light, then heavy gloves over our vulnerable, unprotected skin.

In the fall I tend to want to crawl far back in the Hobbit hole, curl up and read books for the entire winter. The coming bitter cold leaves my fingertips ghostly white, drained of all their warm blood, a remnant of too many near frostbit digits during extreme exposure. The mother of my children and I tend to argue more during the fall months too. We argue about these two very different lifestyles we each want to lead.

She purchased a small farmette about 10 years ago, which was a great place to raise 2 kids. They got to have nearly every animal in the book, gathered warm eggs in the morning and trained dogs on sunny afternoons. Now the kids have grown and moved on and she has enough equity in the house that she is thinking of renting it out and buying a small piece of land in order to create a simpler life.

The other night we were talking about realtors and land speculation and did agree about one thing. We were wondering why all these dingy little shacks that were built in the 20's and 30's are so expensive. When you think about it, all those boards and shingles and glass and doors and wiring and plumbing pipes are very old and were paid for years and years ago. Certainly they all had a worth when they were brand new. But why are these conglomerations of

the exercise tree, leaves falling, and houses across the river

the Kids' house

old materials worth more today than when they were built 70 years ago?

When crawling under her house to do some repairs we see a disastrous maze of pipes and wiring, funky foundation parts and unprofessional add-ons. So what makes this mess worth more and more each year? The land itself could certainly appreciate in value, that's understandable, but to spend all that money, to go into such enormous debt to buy someone else's idea of a home, especially after various owners have added on and made it even more of a mess, doesn't make any sense to us. After these kinds of discussions she's now turned her eye to bare ground and is looking at a tiny piece that lies just down river from my place. She says she wants to build her idea of a dream house there.

You'll remember that one book I mentioned called *The Hobbit* that started me to dreaming over 30 years ago. We joined the masses recently and went to see the *Lord of The Rings* movies, twice! I was so enthralled by the short takes showing those amazing Hobbit houses that I snuck a camera in and snapped the shutter whenever they appeared on screen.

With the flash off of course! Later on I glued these pictures in my scrapbook and kept looking at the unique designs over and over again.

At the time a friend was in the process of building a big underground green house. He told me how he had been taking a trailer into the nearby canyon and bringing back amazing lichen covered boulders. There were green, yellow and orange rocks that he reassembled according to their colors back at the site. In visiting the greenhouse I fell in love with the cliff-like walls he had created. That next spring, just as the snow was melting away, I was too excited to wait until summer, so I made many trips into the hills and canyon lands to the east, hauling back trunkload after trunkload of those beautiful stones. Down off the slippery trail I'd go, sliding to the bottom where I dropped the rocks in a big pile near the doorway, then huffed it back up for more. Soon there were enough for the task and I began placing them, colors matching, all over the front of my tiny abode. I had decided to spruce up the front to make it look like an actual Hobbit house.

Today is Thursday. Its the day that i chased down all of Shilo's chickens and clipped their wings so they couldn't fly over the fence and poop all over the yard any more. Now there's feathers all over the yard and about eleven rilly pissed off chickens.

I then scrounged around and found a pile of old boards, about seven short poles and some used shingles and rebuilt the roof with an overhang, creating a new place to put shoes and to keep the snow away from the front door. Once finished, squirrels began to sit on the pole ends to nibble on their cones and I could hang my coat and hat there as a convenience.

And life went on. Eventually the kids graduated from High School and as I said, moved on to faster paced and more interesting places. I got tired of trying to do odd jobs for people and took a new position as caretaker for the local cemetery. That kept me home and traveling less. And with those changes the meadow seemed to make a big sigh of relief. "Maybe that fool's done now and we

sleeping quarters during the summer

can all rest in peace," it seemed to be saying.

After years and years I finally found the best place to hang the hammock. While swinging there in the shade during the summer months I devour books and write in the journal. Nearby is a flat spot under a fir tree that has become the official "best tent site." For the last two summers a tent set up there has been my cozy bedroom. The cool nights promote deep sleeps. Sometimes I forget the headlamp and have to carefully find the tent in absolute darkness, grabbing for recognizable shrubs and small trees along the winding path as I go. One quiet night as I was laying there in the dusk with my feet hanging out of the tent door I felt a slight brushing and looked up to see a skunk sniffling at my toes then wandering off! The absolute best time is waking up on sunny mornings when the nearby weeds become changing shadows on the tent wall. With each sleepy awakening the scene looks entirely different and you marvel at it until the rising sun makes the tent too hot and you crawl out into the damp grass to start the new day.

looking up the trail to the road

Most tasks in the meadow are now smaller. I built a couple of chairs for sitting around the fire out of driftwood found at the lake. Each fall a tree of delicious yellow plums ripen and I dry about 5 gallons for year round consumption.

Leaves get raked and added to the compost bin or are left to blow away down river. I plant grass seed each spring and dig unwanted weeds out of the small terraced garden on the north end each summer. And slowly but surely the slowed down life I've been dreaming about for so many years peeps out here and there and says Boo!

I have to pinch myself when sitting on the hill looking down at that secret, unseen and seemingly unwanted place. A simple old horse pasture it is. Everyone above me and out across the river want houses and toilets and rattling garbage cans and doorbells. To have found a way to avoid all that extraneous stuff that keeps me separated from pure seeing, pure feeling, seems like a miracle. Sitting there I come to feel a wonderful, unexplainable togetherness that I find no where else in the world. I'm asked to come crawl through the tall grass. To immerse myself in the cool flowing liquid of the river. The very dirt invites me in and I realize that all these elements surrounding me are made of the

(I touch the trees and thank them for their endless patience, their unmoving and solid steadfastness.)

128

 same stuff as me. I just happen to be one of the lucky animate ones that can move around on this earth. I touch the trees and thank them for their endless patience, their unmoving and solid steadfastness. I look up to the mountain and acknowledge its Buddha-like posture, its geologic time frame that makes my life seem like dust in a minute wind. Maybe in a way the land has transformed me back to being at least part animal again, tiny little cells have somehow mutated back to my most primitive past. When sitting quietly in this way I feel a perfect peace in this imperfect and seemingly crazy world.

But hold it! Just as I was thinking about the benefits of early retirement, or of filling that room with enough books so that I may never come out again (local artist passes away reading Faulkner's *As I Lay Dying*), or creating a new occupation called "River Watcher" or "Trail Walker," I was hit with one more grand building idea! And it came in the spring!

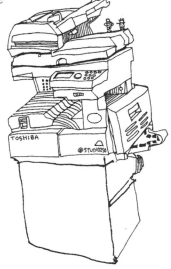

For several months that new copier I had purchased sat lonely, far away in a shed at Lynne's place. To make up some of my *Chronicles* I'd have to ride the 6 miles down there then haul the half-made books back to the meadow and fold and staple them on the carpeted floor of my tiny room. I had recently reissued all the back issues so had stacks of them stuffed on a shelf there too. For years I had been running the business from that room and things were getting a little crowded.

One evening I was out looking at a flat spot along the hillside that I always thought would be a great building site. That night I pulled all the Hand-Made Houses books off the shelf and began to dream and draw plans for a new studio to house the copy machine and all those magazines!

I wrote a letter to the landowners explaining the need for yet another building on their property. You know what their response was. I thanked them. My family thanks them. I think even the universe is probably thanking them, for allowing this nutty person to run through 10-years of alternative living experiments on their land. Such an exceptional gift is so rare in these times of greed and mistrust.

For the next two months, as I was in no hurry and spent endless hours trying to envision the structure, I took pick and shovel to the site and hand dug out a neat 10 X 12 X 4 foot deep slot, throwing all the dirt out front to form a berm that I thought

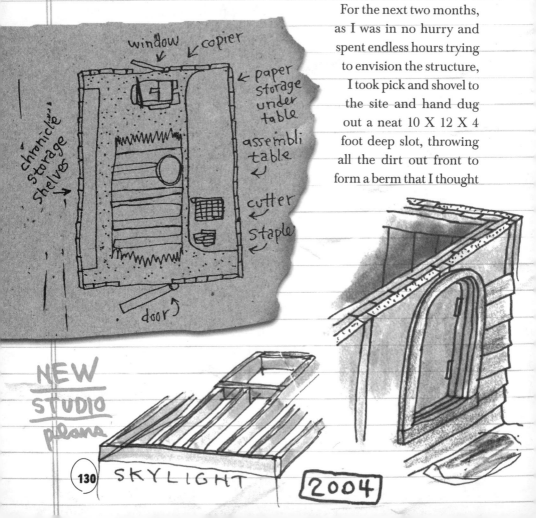

window ← ← copier

← paper storage under table

chronicle storage shelves

assembli table ←

cutter ←

staple ←

door ⌐

NEW STUDIO plans

SKYLIGHT

2004

would hide the building and make it less noticeable.

Having the idea come in the springtime was a blessing as it meant that I had an entire warm season in which to complete the project instead of rushing through it with frozen fingers in the snow. And throughout the entire process I took a different tact than I had on all the other previous buildings. Instead of madly driving around searching for the first recycled materials I could find, I sat back and calmly waited for them to come to me. After all those years of alternative building I knew that if I was patient enough everything needed would appear in due time.

I had just spent the previous eight months helping my son weld

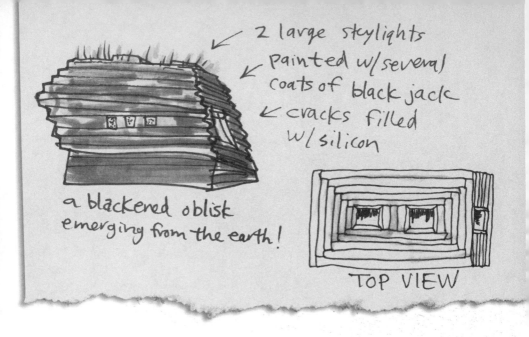

2 large skylights

painted w/several coats of black jack

cracks filled w/silicon

a blackened oblisk emerging from the earth!

TOP VIEW

together a 26 foot scrap metal eagle for his High School. While there I kept noticing three large bunks of 4 X 4 beams that were piled nearby. I finally asked the maintenance man what they were going to do with them and he said that they were mostly rotten and were going to be burned. After closer inspection, not only did I discover them to be mostly solid but I figured the partially rotten ones could be sawed up for firewood as well. A deal was cut. I could have all the wood but I had to get it out of there before the new school year began in the fall.

So after several pickup loads to my place and some dusty chainsaw work I had all the wood I needed to build the new studio, plus about one cord of wood for Lynne's stove. All for free!

After much scribbling I started with a rough plan. I leveled the

site dug out completely

ground and laid three treated 2 X 4's directly on the ground that had been covered in plastic, then screwed down rows of boards to form a floor. I did the leveling work first because all previous structures had been built without the aid of squares or levels. When I set a pencil on the desk in the beach shack it would actually roll off!

As with all other prior projects I didn't have to get a building permit because I was creating such a small structure. And as before I lined the walls, floor and roof with super heavy plastic and tar paper to seal out the moisture. This building was also sunken three feet into the ground so I painted the entire thing with tar when finished. We'll see if those dastardly ants have a taste for that!

After sketching out several different ideas for the wall construction I settled on laying the 4 X 4's up log-cabin-style. Each piece was predrilled and locked in place with long ring shank nails. And instead of just making a boring square coffin-like box I pushed each beam in or out about an inch, causing the walls to undulate and appear to move.

Each exterior crack was sealed with liquid tar and brown silicon filled the inside seams. The entire roof was built from 4 X 4's as well and an extra large (man that sucker's heavy) skylight was welded together to fill the room with light from above. Aside from three small portholes on the front that were finished off with glass cubes on the inside there were no other windows. This design of course deters would-be-robbers, which I'm not real fond of, and also creates a space where there are absolutely no distractions. I can go in there and print and staple nearly a hundred magazines and not even notice an entire day has passed. That's my kind of work space. Plus the phone isn't quite hooked up right yet and only makes outgoing calls!

PHASES OF CONSTRUCTION

A few friends dropped by to see my progress from time to time. Shane helped dig on the hole for about 2 hours one day. I paid him $25. Lynne stays very busy in the summers and helped to dig once for a short while. But other than that, this was an entirely solo creation. Soon the walls rose from the soil and before I knew it the roof was on. After sealing all those joints I sploshed on a thick coating of tar to the outside and sat back staring at it wondering, "Now what?" I considered just leaving it a big black obelisk rising from the earth like that strange wall in the movie *2001: A Space Odyssey*. But one of Shane's friends said, " Yeh that'd be cool, but wouldn't it start melting and smell real bad on hot days?" He was right so I kept making notes late into the night, trying to figure out how to cover the walls so they looked like they belonged there on that sunny hillside.

My buddy up on the hill was getting ready to redo his roof and said I could have all the old cedar shakes I wanted, so that was a possibility. Some of the coolest buildings I've seen are covered from head to toe in randomly laid shingles. While waiting for his roofing contractor to show up I took the dilemma into the sweat lodge each night and thought real hard on it. Still nothing seemed to present itself. Possibly The Old Man was far away working on other building problems.

shingle idea

Then one night while pouring water over the hot rocks I had thoughts about all the rocks I was sitting on and all the rocks spread around the meadow and in the river. And it occurred to me that if done correctly I could cover the entire wooden structure with those rocks, using no mortar to hold it together. Maybe slightly sloping walls and precision fits could make it possible.

That next morning I was up with the birds, slowly levering the largest boulder that had come out of that hand dug hole into place at the

the finished
rock work

base of one wall. Leaving several feet of space between it and the building I shoveled dirt in and laid another, then another, and before long had the front side lined with all the biggest rocks and filled in. It looked like a planter. And so it went, me going to every rock pile I'd made in the meadow and packing them back up the small hill and placing them on the wall. The sandy soil worked perfect as uncemented mortar, filling in all the cracks and settling in to form a secure base for the stones. Up and up it went. And as I worked I remembered a story I'd read in the old Shelter book from the 1970's. One of the builders explained that the first thing you need to do on a new site is look at all the resources that are there very carefully. Then try to utilize all the materials that are naturally at hand in your building. That way you don't have to pack in a bunch of alien parts and pieces, and your finished creation looks like it grew there.

From the very beginning, I had always strived for a lifestyle and living spaces that were as invisible as possible. During that entire summer I was beset with worries that the new studio was going to stand out too much. I thought maybe I should have dug it deeper into the ground somehow. In fact there were days when I wished I had just dug a deep

THE FRONT SIDE

enough hole that the whole thing was buried with only a skylight at ground level. But it was too late to go back. Laying up the rock was definitely the most exciting thing I'd ever done. After each round of stones I'd stand back and smile wide at the utter organicness of it. It looked like some rediscovered Incan ruin or Pueblo Indian kiva rising there on the side of the hill in the dappled sunlight. And what a joy it was to work in T-shirt and sandals.

On I worked for over a month finding all the stray boulders and rocks I could squeeze out of the land. In the end I drove down the county roads picking up the last ones needed to finish off the roof area. And I think that was the hardest work I've ever done—moving big rock after big rock down off the steep hillside, sweating away in that hot August heat, then climbing directly back up again to carry more back down.

The bulging corners were pushed out to create a solid looking foundation much like the buildings I'd seen on the rim of the Grand Canyon years earlier. The skylight filled the new room with a glow that I had encountered when entering the sacred kivas in the southwest. And the door was made from several thick weathered planks that I had rescued from the burn pile at the cemetery.

It was kind of weird sitting in that brand new place after a day of hard work. I'd look up through the window at the big pines waving on the windy hill. Weird because here I had taken this space in the trees. That once empty spot below the towering cottonwood, and created an entirely different space. An enclosure that was roofed in. A cave. A tomb. For the

first time ever it felt strange to have converted what was once just open land to this solid, immovable object. Maybe what was digging at me is that this heavy structure, because of how it had been so majorly nailed together and secured from the elements would probably end up being there for many, many years to come. Way longer even than I would be alive.
So that got me to worrying about what would become of it long after I was dead and gone. Never before had I constructed such a lasting thing in the meadow. But don't worry, I didn't burn it down.

That first roof I built leaked like a sieve. So I totally removed it and started over again. I'd recommend to anyone building a flat roof structure to put at least a slight slope on it as flat roofs with skylights are almost impossible to seal. The second try was a success. I then covered the whole thing with dirt hauled bucket by bucket from that berm out front. Another agonizingly strenuous endeavor. Grass seed was sown and watered each day, and a few months later it looked as if the rock house had been there since the beginning of time.

Now all my little Chronicles are made right there, with no need to haul anything anywhere. I have space to fill all the orders and do the mail. And just like the Hobbit house, the new studio is easily heated with just a small ceramic stove that costs about 25 cents a day.

And even though I know deep in my bones that all the

handmade rock shelter I built on the Baja coast

the first camp out
and plans

experiments in that wondrous place are now completed, I do have one last dream that has been working its way to the front of my mind for many years. Just as wealthy folks build new homes in several different locales, I've always wanted to build little secret hideaways in other places, so that I could return there with a few weeks of food in a pack to stay for awhile. For a change of scenery. For a vacation.

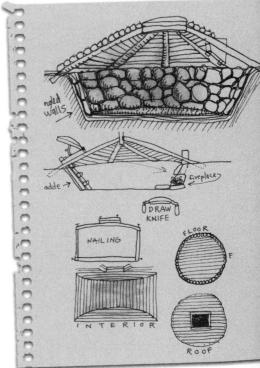

The first such abode was built on a wild shoreline on the coast of Baja in the mid 90's. Eventually I went back to visit the place with the family and discovered it had been torn down. Then two years ago as I lay sick in bed looking at a topographical map with a big magnifying glass, I spotted a remote flat spot on a mountainside not far from home. Once healthy I strapped on the trusty snowshoes and made tracks up a nearly vertical slope, pulling

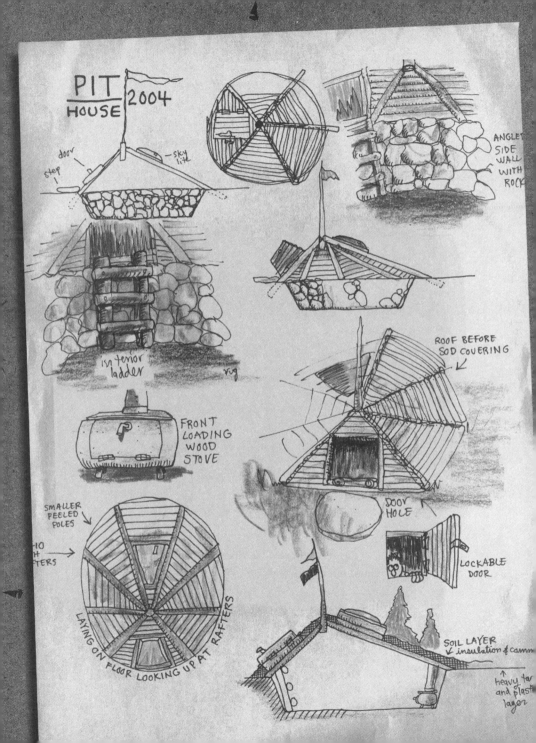

myself up and over the edge on long tree limbs to discover another absolutely stunning location.

Since that day I've pitched the tent there many times, hanging out, watching and looking, knowing that one day I would figure out what the place wanted me to do there. I envisioned making a small lean to that had some sort of fire source inside for comfortable winter visits. Then this last summer I found a few open days from my busy life at the cemetery and began laying up some of the downed poles in the area. On the back side lies a huge field of flat stones, so I hauled pieces over and built a rock fireplace in one end . The ideas continue to come.

Sometimes late at night I'll hear a distant voice and have to get up to write down what it's saying. I often wonder will it ever end?. How many more such forts and club houses will I build? Will I ever just finally grow up and leave all this child-like business behind? But most importantly I always ask myself, and The Old Man too, have I indeed lived a life at all like my ancient ancestors?. Did I honor this land, and have I lived on it in the least damaging and most respectable way possible? How will I ever know? Who can I ask that could tell me? Will any of us find true peace on this earth we call home?

. . .so far this is
what I've built

door ↗

WILL ANY OF US FIND TRUE PEACE ON THIS EARTH WE CALL HOME?

THE
END
OF THE
BEGINNINGS

"IF SOMEONE ASKED ME WHAT I REALLY WANTED in this life, I'd have to say freedom. Just plain old fashioned, home-made, living in a tent, fishing lots, one meal a day, big walk abouts, healthy, happy, book reading, scribbling crazy notes about this wild world, wondering about stuff, playing in the mud, shooting marbles, drawing all the 10,000 things, cat petting, sleeping in, freedom . . . yeh!"

—Moonlight Chronicles, 1997

Some of us are born with unrealizable and unattainable dreams. They push and pull our beings through life like a pack of wild dogs on the end of a hundred straining leashes. But just coming to realize that some of those dreams could be a reality can be the first big step in a persons coming of age. Then comes an even scarier part, where those subtle voices that emanate from hidden pockets in the universe all around, ask you to step off cliffs! Having the guts to do that may be the biggest test of all. It seems that everywhere some of us look we see hints and signs of a better way. A way that is however contrary to the accepted "belief system." Many and even most of your family and friends will contend that the safest course lies with the herd. "Security" is coveted like an Olympic flame and carried aloft for all to see. "Conventionality" has become societies mantra scratched deep and hard in stone.

There are a few new pioneers however. Souls who feel the pull of the cliff's edge more keenly and when no one is looking, leap off, falling, falling. It is the most free they ever feel. But don't search for their remains there amongst the boulders below, because the very faith that convinced them to jump from that precipice, quietly caught them half way down and took them to a

the sweatlodge

whole new place. A new world bright with endless possibility. A land where fear is welcomed and walked into rather than avoided. These people discover an unknown secret about life and are forever changed. Some have become legends. Some simply die.

I can finally and only relax when I feel a sense of singularity with things. Through these many and extensive studies into the realm of neo-lifestyles, I have found that a single human being can live comfortably and both healthy and happy, in an 80 square foot space, nestled like a river otter in its burrow. Surely this seems highly unlikely to modern day folks who not only live in 2500 square foot houses today, but actually dream of someday getting a 10,000 square foot or even larger homes. But, I'm wondering, just how many building resources will we be allowed to take before there isn't anything left for future generations?

That tiny nest of mine on the river contains all that I own. Most of it would fit in a good sized pickup truck. My bed is a simple three-inch foam pad given to me by a friend. The bedding consists of one large and

THE INTERIOR OF THE HOBBIT HOLE...

very cozy sleeping bag! No sheets or bulky comforters to argue with on restless nights. In this simple sleeper I sleep the sleep of the dead. And all those cliffs I walked off, in the end, revealed truths as simple as that. When you're willing to give something up the rewards you receive are always way more interesting than what you had. Go find a truly comfortable sleeping bag and you may never return to the land of bed making again!

More stories. After keeping all my pitiful sums of money in the local bank for the last 14 years, I went in to see about a loan to purchase a $5000 copier that I desperately needed for my micro-magazine business. I had been going to the nearby Copy Club for years then realized one day that I'd save a bunch of money if I owned my own machine. The banker sat like a stuffed shirt in a tight tie that seemed to be choking him. And after some investigations into my "borrowable equity," he announced

my only apparent equity!

I actually didn't have any! And that even though I'd been a faithful customer for all those years, the bank wasn't really interested in "making a loan for a copier." The fact that I had virtually a non-existent credit record and no real possessions of value that they could hold as collateral, seemed to be the central deciding factors. Bummer.

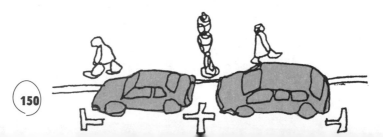

So I sadly rode away on my only apparent equity, a $500 mountain bike, from all that official uptightness and contracts and money talk, and sat in The Old Man's steam for an evening to find a better answer. The next morning I was on the phone to a wealthy friend in New York City who said yes, of course he'd loan me the money, and at no interest to boot! Along with the check that arrived a few days later was a hilarious note explaining the monthly payment schedule and the fatal consequences if I failed to come through on my end! He would fly in to repossess my beloved Hobbit Hole!!

The reason I'm telling you this story is because it's a good example of how a person *could* be living. Rather than dealing in those dastardly, dreaded contract signings, that basically explain how the lending insti-

tution is going to make tons of money in interest off your little transaction. Plus if you look closely at the fine print, you'll notice the clause explaining that after they do this they'll be needing the shirt off your back as well!

Yet the transaction made with my friend was not only pleasant and non-threatening (he never did ask me what my net worth was, as if that

has anything to do with my actual real worth as a human being), but ended up being fun and exciting as well. It's remembered in the little noggin up there as a good experience. It endears me further to my friend. And it makes me want to somehow return the favor.

Now when I go into the bank I park my bike outside, inhale deeply of all that fresh air I've been enjoying, and feel sorry for Mr. Banker, pinned to his chair there underneath all those fluorescent lights. Of course the point of my story is to remind you that there are other ways of doing business. Some people love to barter. Others will trade favors like my friend did. It's also a reminder of how steering clear of unnecessary contracts can actually create a less complicated and happier life.

Of course the main idea behind all this seeming madness is to just go in the opposite direction from everyone else. To search far and wide for more cliff edges, to see just how minimal a person can be. All in the name of freedom. And not to just engage in some momentary weird experiment, but to discover an authentic state of true freedom, where no one is directing your actions. If you feel like reading all day, great. If you decide to make bicycles your main mode of transportation, awesome. No one is bringing you long lists of things that need doing. (good luck on this one all you married guys. My buddy and I finally realized the "honey-do list" is not on single sheets but actually an endless roll of paper!) Ha.

Like some old hobo on a rickety train car going headlong into the mist, with no destination, no schedules, not even knowing where he'll end up. That's the idea. Just letting the entire weird world go flowing on by like some rowdy river. Sitting back, watching it go. Freedom has got to be one of the toughest concepts to define. But isn't it what they say America was founded on?

I thought I'd conclude this book with some of the ideas I've come across that you may also want to try. And at the risk of making it sound too much like some looney penny pincher, lets begin with a quote from that famous guru of a ski film maker Warren Miller, "If you're not around the back trying to figure out a way to get in free, you're paying too much!" Which reminds me of an old advertisement I saw in an outdoor magazine. Picture this. A photo of an old beater pickup truck. In the back was a new pair of down hill skis. The headline read something like, "College education? Important job? New house? We all make mistakes!" Ha. In my book the owner definitely had his priorities straight.

Here's a few tidbits to get you going in a simpler direction. Crumbs that may get you to baking some cookies:

1. LAWNS

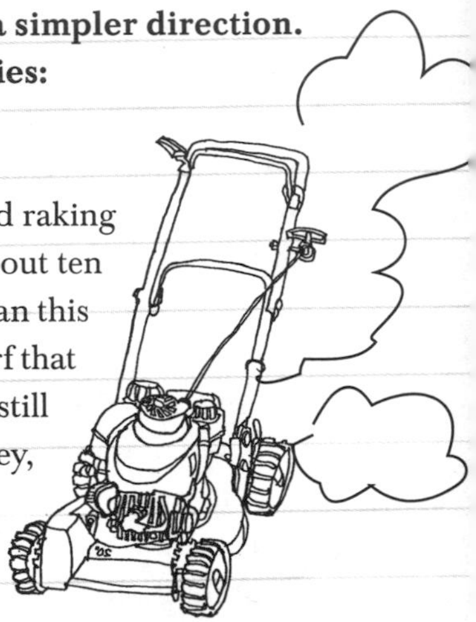

I just finished mowing and raking my entire lawn. It took about ten minutes. And I enjoyed every one of them. How can this be, you ask? Well, do you own a huge expanse of turf that won't leave you alone all summer long? "We're still growing! Isn't it time for another trim now? And hey, how about another dose of that yummy fertilizer while you're at it. Make it the kind with some weed killer on the side, will ya? Those guys are sooo annoying!"

old smokey

You know how expensive lawns can be. There's the watering, the mower, and now gas is over $2 a gallon! Plus the unseemly fact that you're out there spewing noxious fumes all over the neighborhood and contributing to noise pollution as well. Sheesh, and all for a pretty lawn.

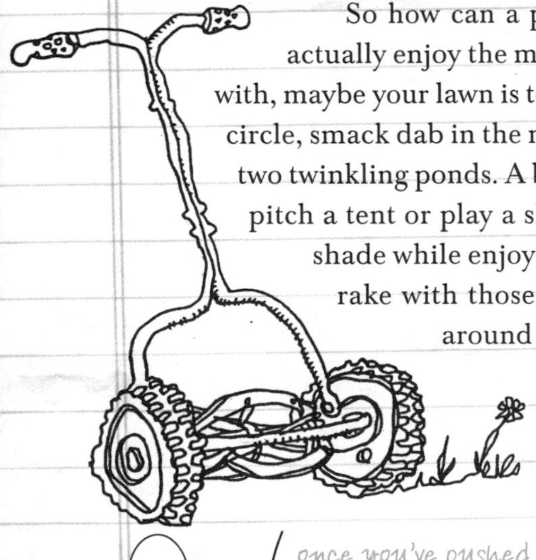

So how can a person avoid all that nastiness and actually enjoy the maintenance of a yard? Well, to begin with, maybe your lawn is too damn big!! Mine is a mere 30 foot circle, smack dab in the middle of the meadow. Right next to two twinkling ponds. A beautiful place for visiting friends to pitch a tent or play a slow game of croquet in the evening shade while enjoying a cold drink. There's an antique rake with those cool old school metal tines hiding around there somewhere that I got at a yard sale for a buck. And my pride and joy, a *push* mower, that devours no gas or oil and happily clips along going clackety-clack, while I get a

(once you've pushed a motor-less mower while enjoying the birdsong overhead you may never climb on "ole smokey" again.)

little exercise in the bargain. What a deal!

When the kids spent those summers in the tipi, I'd mow in the early mornings going round and round our circular home singing, "Ya gotta get up, ya gotta get up, ya gotta get up this morning..."

So somehow you 've got to downsize. Put in a garden. Tell your neighbor he can have most of your lawn! But seriously, once you've pushed a motor-less mower while enjoying the birdsong overhead you may never climb on "ole smokey" again.

2. WATERING

Once again my partner and I are on opposite ends on this one. She's hooked up to the city water meter system and receives large water bills each and every month. I fill buckets from the river and dump them on thankful trees and bushes. She also tends to buy those new fangled plastic hose sprayers that leak, soak your clothes and end up breaking after only one season. I'm still using an old brass nozzle I found ten years ago. Go figure.

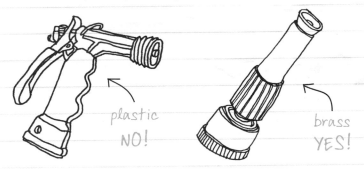

plastic
NO!

brass
YES!

3. CLOTHES

Sure, there's nothing like the feel of pulling on a brand new pair of pants, shirt, or shoes, right? But I'd like to know why people have entire closets full of these body coverings? Of course we all need some variety, but it almost seems like some people are afraid of

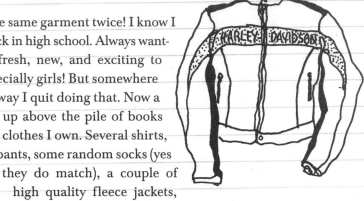

being seen in the same garment twice! I know I was that way back in high school. Always wanting to appear fresh, new, and exciting to others, especially girls! But somewhere along the way I quit doing that. Now a small shelf up above the pile of books holds all the clothes I own. Several shirts, three pair of pants, some random socks (yes they do match), a couple of high quality fleece jackets,

and two caps and a pair of wool gloves. I say covering up your skin doesn't have to be expensive. Many perfectly good shirts can be found at second hand and Goodwill stores. And if you live in a college town you'll be amazed at what those youngsters toss off. And another thing about having less clothes? You never face the dilemma of what to wear, because your choices are so few! Ha. I win.

4. THE WASH

It's been our experience all along, especially since having teenagers, that the more clothes you have, the more wash you do! Strange isn't it how these young people think that one day in a pair of pants while sitting reading books in class necessitates an immediate trip through the wash and spin cycle? Those measly three pair of mine are worn until they are dirty! And then washed.

When not at the kids' house (helping to do all that wash), I head off on my bike to the local wash house near my place and enjoy conversation with complete strangers while the clothes scrub and tumble for about an hour. In the summer months I bring them back to the meadow still wet and hang them on a long blue line to dry in a rustling breeze.

5. FOOD

Now I may be getting ready to put my foot in my mouth on this one. Okay, look. How many of you love to eat out at the coolest restaurant in town? Raise your right hands. Yes, I'm seeing lots of hands. Undoubtedly one of man's favorite pastimes, right? And one that many people extend into their own homes via fancy cookbooks and pricey cookware. Eating is of course something we all must do. But let me challenge you a bit on this one. I'd like to know who came up with this whole system called Breakfast, Lunch and Dinner? Doctors are now suggesting that we eat less since the obesity rate went from 25% to 65% in the last 20 years! Hello. We could all get along with eating way less and when we do eat to have smaller portions. So tone it down a bit on the intake and maybe you'll actually appreciate your food more. Someone said that the longest lived people on the earth are the bushmen of Africa. You've seen them. Gaunt, skinny as bean poles. Apparently they are almost always hungry. But they live to be the oldest of all us overfed, over-everything consumers.

Some years ago I ran across some books by Harlan Hubbard and learned about how he and his wife who spent the last 40 years of their lives eating simply from their garden, the river, and whatever else they could barter or hunt for.

While getting into the backpack traveling mode in the 90's I was amazed at all the high tech gizmos and gadgets stores were selling so that people could eat like kings in the backcountry. Right away I decided, "Hold on just a minute," The reason I was going somewhere with a pack on my back was precisely to *get away* from all the trappings of homes and kitchens.!

So instead of buying a pile of expensive mini stoves, and non stick pots and pans, then slaving away at cooking big meals and cleaning up that whole big mess in the woods, I developed a strict NO COOKING policy in regards to eating. Although I figured if I was dumb enough to carry in a heavy can of beans on my aching back then I could easily pop the top and heat it by the flames of a bright and cheery fire, hobo-style. And for quick overnighters, we usually bring along a package of stew meat that we cook on the end of sticks then sprinkle with salt and pepper, cave man style!

When back in the meadow I continued on with that no cooking policy and only occasionally heat something up on the hot plate. It's real easy to get your fruit, vegetables, protein and carbs without creating a bunch of messy dishes. Daily vitamins and a piece of dried garlic (the Russians answer to penicillin), round out the mineral needs. Sandwiches are fun. Cereal tastes great. Crackers and cheese are an old outdoorsmen staple. Along with lettuce and bags of those tiny carrots, all this and little else keep this Hobbit's motor chugging along, plenty plump and itchin to get back outside where the real action is taking place! To watch the butterflies in the bushes. The geese honking southwards on chilled winds. All those ants scurrying about.

The plain truth is that we do eat too much. Try fasting for a 24 hour period each week, say from noon on Saturday to noon on Sunday and watch your grocery bill and your belly shrink, while your spirits soar.

6. DRYING FOOD

Take a drive in the countryside in the fall and you'll notice many wild fruit trees lining the roads. In a country where food is literally dropping off the trees, it's hard to believe or even conceive that children and others are going hungry. Over the years I kept running across fruit dryers at yard sales and now own two large size homemade ones. Ones that in a few short days of cutting and spreading, dry enough fruit to nibble on each day until the next season swings around. What's nice about dried foods is that you don't have to refrigerate them, plus they  are extremely light and take up very little space. After deciding back in 1994 to step off a slightly smaller cliff and give up my mini refrigerator, I have utilized dry foods as much as possible. Our favorite is jerky, made by cutting thin strips of meat, soaking it in

a tasty, salty brine, then carefully drying it to the point of perfection. One trip to any library will probably net you all the books you'll ever need on how to get started.

Hunting is a practice I've always been interested in, but have yet to learn. Many friends get a deer or elk each year for some extraordinary tasting meat. They tell me of the strong bond they feel with the land and those animals who give of their own lives in order to nourish other beings.

7. GARDENS

If you walk northwards in the meadow, you'll come across a large mossy rock on the right that lies next to a tiny stream of water filled with watercress. On the left are several terraces carved into a steep hillside that I've been growing lettuce and spinach on for four years. I enjoy stopping my bike to pick a big handful of the greens, washing them in the nearby clear water and gobbling them whole. Salad doesn't get any fresher than that.

If your climate is warm enough you ought to take some time to experience growing some of your own food. Not only are you guaranteed some pure and organic nutrition but you'll also be benefiting from getting your hands in the soil and feeling the absolute naturalness of the entire process. We should all have the skills and know the joys of growing vegetables. Someone recently said that it ought to be a mandatory class in school. That all children should be taught how to create a garden. That way if some disaster did happen, most of us would know how to feed ourselves. Novel idea, huh?

If you have a sunny window in your home, why not build a miniature greenhouse for a nice row of lettuce? And don't forget how easy sprouts are to grow in a jar. With just a little bit of common sense and attention, we could all be improving the quality of our food intake.

B. BOOKS

I don't know about you, but as much as I love books, I don't usually buy that many. If I do buy one, I'll read it, study it, digest it and let it hang around for awhile. But if it doesn't pass the keeper test, I pass it on to a friend. In the past I've also used inter-library loan systems to get hard-to-find books. Check with your local library to see if they offer this service for a nominal fee.

Please don't even get me started on books vs. TV. Back in the day, we all watched a lot of TV, especially the educational channel. But then we made an interesting discovery. We were surprised to find that we were sitting through entire programs and only towards the end realizing we had actually already seen them before!

Don't even get me started on books vs. TV

Scientists know why this happens. Apparently when you watch TV you are what's known as a "passive" observer. When in this passive state it's been proven that you are NOT learning. Books on the other hand cause us to use our own imaginations, creating whole scenarios in our heads as we read along. This is good. This is stimulating those tweaky neurons and getting them to exercise a bit. TV just hands them a bowl of crackers and says, "party on dude." With a television you just turn it on, chow on the chips and are entertained by whatever mindless thing happens to be dancing across the screen. I'm always so dismayed when out walking the neighborhood at night to see just how many homes embrace that eerie glow. So hooray for books! May we always be able to spend intimate time with them even with that maniacal digital world blasting away in the other room.

9. JOURNALING

If you try and adopt a more simplified way of living and actually do make some leaps into that new way of being, you may find yourself a bit bored with all that extra time you have. That's where keeping a journal of your activities can become a real bonus. If you are still tied inextricably to the 9 to 5 and a full-blown home, and don't have time for a daily journal, maybe you could begin a garden journal, or even a dream journal. Some people simply write down all the funny things their young children say. We always kept a tape recorder on the kitchen table when the kids were little and pushed the record button whenever they started talking. Those tapes are among our most prized possessions now. The whole point is to realize that your own life is important and definitely worth documenting in some form or other. There are those lucky few who do eventually decide to make a leap of faith and get that often-dreamed-of 'cabin in the woods.' Unfortunately they are so used to being busy 24-7 that once they get there they become restless and bored, not knowing what to do with all those free hours. But if you take up journaling and practice the fine art of being an astute observer of life, then those boring days soon become filled with interesting things for you to document. Sketching and painting and carrying a drawing book with you at all times can also make you look at the world in a whole new way. Once you begin you'll be amazed at how filled the world is with interesting things and how much you've been missing all these years being "busy."

10. RECYCLING

By now you've probably figured out that I'm not the kind of guy who has an architect draw up some fancy plans then calls the lumber yard to order piles of new building materials. If you spend some time looking around for free and unused material you'll be amazed at how much there is. I have a friend who after making a few phone calls secured enough lumber to build entire buildings. Granted he did have to be willing to disassemble a couple of old homes and barns, which was a lot of work. But the wood was still highly usable and knot free, coming from those old growth forests years ago. Placing an ad in your local newspaper will sometimes generate more calls than you can deal with. It seems there's lots of people out there who want their old piles of boards gone for good and will say they are free for the hauling.

Just to cover the small area in front of my place with paving stones would have cost several hundred dollars I'm guessing. Luckily I had asked about the discarded pieces from a sidewalk project up town several years ago and discovered that they were being hauled away to a landfill nearby. Many of them are odd shaped, but that just made piecing them back together all the more fun. In the end the scrambled shapes look more organic and natural than the rows and rows of perfectly square ones on main street.

While visiting larger cities I've even seen whole companies that are in the business of tearing down old structures and reselling the used lumber. And in many cases, the weatherworn and faded boards are more attractive looking than stark new ones.

Last year after a long hard day at the cemetery I came back home and had the urge to rebuild the tiny dock on the river. Towards the end I ran out of nails and was too tired to ride uptown to buy a bag of new owns, so carefully straightened out all the rusty ones I had pulled out of the old boards and reused them! Pretty ridiculous, I know, but those rusty nails will hold the dock together for a few more years when I'll have the pleasure once again of adding other boards to the dock. More than likely some beautiful driftwood ones I happened upon along the lake shore.

11. CARS vs. BIKES

In a perfect world of course, all human locomotion would be self-generated. Our caloric intake would equal the number of pedal rotations we could do each day and auto pollution would be nonexistent. In that perfect world people would be less stressed and healthier because they had exercised more in order to get from here to there. Bicycles would be attached to small generators so that someone in the family would have to pedal before all the gadgets worked. Instead of gorging on beer and snacks, all those fat guys would be pedaling and trim in order to watch all those games on the television! Kids would be strapped in to keep the washers and dryers going and even the computer would require an exercise quota that had to be met before it even came on! I wonder how many of those kids zoned out on videos game would just go outside to play instead?

While on a bike ride across the state of Oregon I ran across a guy who was living in a tent near a small town. He cooked all his meals over a fire and was in definite need of a long, hot shower. But he said some-

thing that I'll probably never forget. He said, looking up at all the passing cars, "Look at them. What are they all gonna do when the gas runs out? None of their motors will run. They won't even be able to mow their stupid lawns, the fools." And I had to agree with him. He had a good point. Even though most of us are tied to our cars and couldn't live our lives without them, how is it that we can continue purchasing even larger ones, spew tons of pollutants onto our precious planet, and feel okay about that? Have you ever ran a lawn mower inside a garage for a few minutes? How about a car? Within less than a minute you can't even breathe. The fumes are so strong that you begin choking. And some folks, tired of living, actually find a relatively easy way out by sitting in the garage with the door closed and their car running. Are we tired of living too? It's madness, and anyone who has spent any time at all on a bike, will tell you how incredibly rude an automobile feels as it blasts past you at 60mph, scattering all the wild life, ruining the pure air. So don't we all need to get on bikes more than we do? It's such a great way to go. You'll be reminded of old and long-forgotten childhood pleasures. You'll actually smell things and feel your muscles grow and you'll be able to stop and talk to people on the sidewalk. I've even met older retired couples out on the road, in the middle of nowhere, who decided to chuck it all, bought touring bikes and bags and are spending the remainder of their years seeing America, on a bike ! Now that's impressive. Certainly better than staring at the T.V. in some old house.

Just the other day I stayed overnight at Lynne's house while she was away on a short business trip. She had been complaining about how quiet it is there, now that the kids are gone. And you know what? She's absolutely right. It's a total lonely-ass place now. There's old family ghosts lurking all around. In every corner. On every shelf. Memories in every room that won't go away. It's sad as hell. Plus, it's a dumb old house. An outdated idea of what a shelter ought to be. It's got way too much space that just fills up with all that stuff. So of course it's lonely! That's how houses are. They suck up all that people energy for years, then seep it back out on the unsuspecting old folks who end up staying there. Making them all crazy and sad. I told Lynne that at this point she needs to go create her own place. Something entirely different in order to create new memories. And the really interesting thing is, my place in the meadow never ever makes me feel sad. So go figure.

Houses suck up all that people energy for years, then seep it back out on the unsuspecting old folks who end up staying there.

WELL, THAT'S IT. I'm done now. I've shared just about everything I know about the simple life. It's actually a very personal journey you know. Different for each one who chooses to walk that uninhabited path. For me it's been a long and sometimes strange journey. Family members questioned my actions all along. It would have been a lot easier to just have stayed in that cabin at the lake, although it has now been torn down, or endured that old brick flophouse hotel room downtown with its noisy nights and dusty corners.

Looking around the meadow this summer, after finishing up the new rock studio, I took this question into The Old Man. Why after making such a monumental discovery about what a person *really* needs to live, couldn't I have just been happy with a little blue tent at the end of a well worn trail down there in that meadow? Why was I called to go buy a tipi and build a wooden floor and then be drug on and on through all those different methods of habitation when a simple tent would have sufficed? Plus I could have had the freedom all those years to do what I've wanted to do all along, which was finally learn how to "do nothing" like the ancient Buddha texts teach?

Sitting in all that heat, sweat streaming off the end of my nose in the darkness, darkness so dark you sometimes feel like a pen being dipped in a deep bottle of black ink, I asked for some reasons why. The hot rocks only spit and sputtered and sent more heat. Just like The Old Man I thought, never responding to a direct question. But later on, while dreaming onward, trying to work out the puzzle of words to this last chapter, he did seem to send an interesting message. First he said to forgive myself for all that experimentation. That the land was simply amused by all my overzealous activities. That old stones don't care where you roll them. That the trees feel your presence but are busy with growing and swimming in the wind. And the dirt, well the dirt has its own world going on of hairy microbes and even tinier microbes on the backs of even smaller and even hairier microbes. It doesn't even perceive being carted around or carried off to new places since for it, all else and everything is just an illusion. All it knows is to compost onward forever.

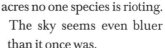

And to the human eye, the meadow is certainly in better shape than when I found it. The grasses are flexing and strong. The bushes sprout new growth after each pruning and stretch their weaving tendrils towards the sun. While across the fence lines bad weeds are partying hard, on these two acres no one species is rioting. The sky seems even bluer than it once was.

How easy life seems now. Like the banker said, I have no equity. That means I'm free from making too many monthly payments for things that I really don't need anyway. And right here in this fine, rolling, wide country of ours, in one of the biggest experimental consumer machines the world has ever seen, sits one tiny being, trying with all his little might to paddle the other way. With no nothing. Just a little food, a few clothes and a cozy shelter. What more do we as people really need?

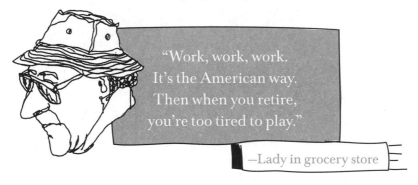

"Work, work, work.
It's the American way.
Then when you retire,
you're too tired to play."

—Lady in grocery store

I'm not real fond of poetry, but for some reason The Old Man left me scrambling for a pen and paper recently. I guess they are going to be the best words I can come up with to bid you good luck and farewell:

Shilo's first driving of the car. Ha.

Finally the end is drawing near,
And I realize that was quite a concoction I brewed up and
poured in your ear.
I'm not here to tell you my life's any better than yours.
It's not my job to convince others to relax and have less chores.
All I know is there's ants down yonder near the elderberry tree.
That there's fish over in the river,
and that bees are free.

I've seen hawks that hover over a tipi with care,
Looking down and calling out whenever I was there.
I've seen old folks visit and be awed by the sights,
I've seen kids swing and bats sing,
alone in the nights.
That flowers are prettiest when growing amongst weeds,
That a free man is a man who can do as he pleases.
That sunsets are serene when seen from afar,
That bugs are interesting when looked at in a jar.
And I know why monks become monks and hoboes ride trains,
Why there's dusty red ponies running free on the plains.
It's because they all discovered something we may never know,
That life isn't about anything, but learning to let go.

—d.price OCTOBER 26, 2005
Joseph, Oregon

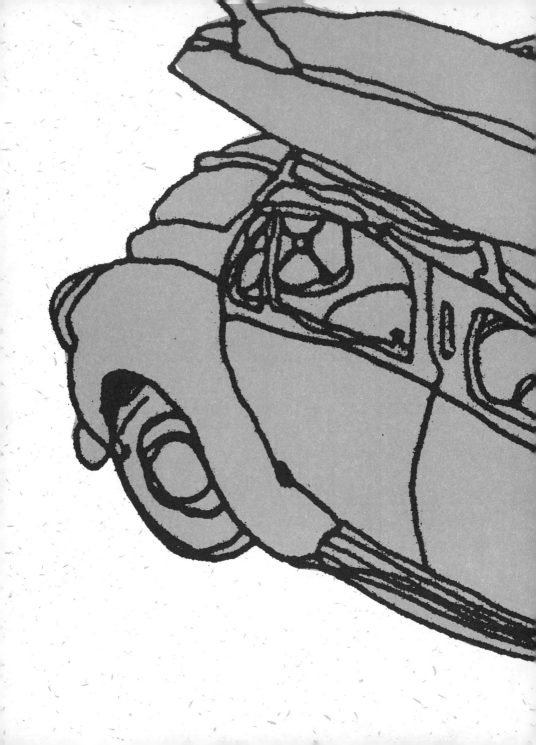

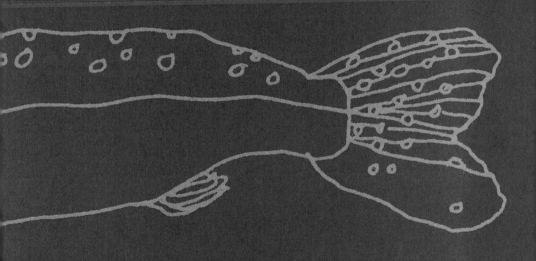

Shane →

← Dan

It's official. Alien beings have contacted earth and they will be by to pick him up any day now. It's all been a big mistake. Somehow he got left behind clear back in 1957. In the meantime he flunked college, took pictures for lots of newspapers, created a photo magazine, then an illustrated journal. He's written books, raised children and been hiding out in an undisclosed meadow in eastern Oregon for years. He's been seen on strange bicycles and currently drives a 1985 tan Astro van. If seen contact the authorities immediatly!

REGISTERED
NOT FROM HERE